A Field Guide for
FAMILIES

A Field Guide for
FAMILIES

How to Assist Your Older Loved Ones
When You Don't Live Next Door

Jane Yousey

Life Design Publishing
Niantic, Connecticut

First printing 2002.
ISBN 0-9716566-0-6

Table of Contents

Dedication

This book is dedicated in memory of my beloved father

Donald Richardson
October 3, 1928—October 14, 2001

And my beloved father-in-law

Edward C. Yousey
February 24, 1916—September 11, 2001

Both men left a legacy of love that will live on eternally

You are an essential piece of the puzzle of humanity...
Once you know who you are and to whom you are
linked, you will know what to do

EPICTETUS 81 AD

Message for Families

Aging. We're all doing it. We are not only trying to age successfully ourselves, but also are trying to assist those we love to do the same. The task is not easy. Frequently, many miles separate us from those we love and seek to help. Family responsibilities, demanding careers, and lack of time all add pressure to our already busy lives. We need help. Direction. We need clarification on when to be concerned and step in, and when to respect independence and hold back. This book was written with a heartfelt desire to help those of us with older loved ones.

A Field Guide For Families helps families learn how and when to help their older loved one. Packed with practical solutions, *A Field Guide For Families* helps families better understand the physical, mental, emotional, and spiritual changes that come with aging. Many families need help to quickly assess and evaluate what is needed. Intended to guide families in knowing what to do and when to step in, this book includes over twenty Checklists for Successful Aging, which provide timely evaluation and solutions for the most difficult challenges to successful aging.

- Recognize that family challenges are not easy. Know Your "Rights."

A Family Member's Bill of Rights

1. You have the right to take the best care of yourself that you possibly can.
2. You have the right to maintain your independence.
3. You have the right to carve out a portion of each day for yourself.
4. You have the right to rely on others to help support your older loved ones.
5. You have the right to have bad days.
6. You have the right to share your responsibilities with others.
7. You have the right to suffer as little as possible.
8. You have the right to set healthy boundaries.
9. You have the right to live free of guilt.
10. You have the right to feel proud of the care and concern you show others.

- **Use Your Time Wisely**
  1. **Plan** to make the most of your visits. Set an agenda for what you wish to accomplish with each visit. Be sure to include fun and enjoyable activities in each visit. Treasure the time you are able to spend together.
  2. **Research** what local services are needed and what services are available in the local community. Start by contacting the community senior center or agency on aging. The Internet is a tremendous source of information for families.
  3. **Listen**. Really listen to what your older loved ones say. Acknowledge resistance when it is present and try to understand the source of the resistance. Is it fear? Is it misunderstanding?

Is it financial concern? Who do your loved ones trust to help them better understand your concerns? Call in a social worker, case manager, trusted friend, or clergy member when appropriate.

4. **Understand** that your goals may be different from theirs. Try to respect your older loved ones' right to autonomy and independence. You can best honor them by helping to make decisions WITH them and not FOR them. How can their needs be met, while at the same time respecting their right to choose?

- **Develop Your Skills in Relating to Older Persons**
  Life does not stand still, but many older folks wish it would. Many seniors long for the "Remember when...?" days – the days when they felt as invincible as we do today. So, how can we honor and connect to these older folks that we love so much?

  1. **Honor Their Wisdom**
     Life is a tremendous teacher. Seniors have been learning for a lot longer than we have.

  2. **Listen With Your Heart**
     Seniors want to be listened to, not just heard. If we listen well enough we can hear the message that they want us to have more than they had. They are trying to tell us HOW. Listen.

  3. **Hear Their Stories**
     Life is a series of stories connecting people, places and experiences. The stories tell of a person's life, dreams, successes, challenges, wins, defeats, and triumphs. An older person's stories are about what made them who they are today. This is the person they want us to know and love.

4. **Trace The Lines Of Their Faces**

   The lines are memories. See the smile lines around their eyes, those we put there with the antics of our childhood. See the lines and marks on their hands? They came with hours of playing catch, pitching tents, making beds, putting up the holiday decorations, assembling bicycles, and building sandcastles with us. Honor older loved ones for what those lines represent.

5. **Know That Older People Are You. Later.**

   They ask themselves, "Wasn't it just yesterday I was that new bride, that new mommy, bought that first home, led that boy scout troop up the hiking trail, drove the children to after-school activities, saw them hit home runs at high school games, packed them up for college, met their "one and onlys," walked them down the aisle, held that first grandchild? Where has the time gone? Who have I become? It seems like just yesterday…"

6. **Understand The Impact Of Loss**

   Aging involves loss. A lot of loss. This may include loss of independence, of friends, of bodily functions, of power, of their own home, of memory, of keen vision, of energy, of time, of hope, of a long future ahead, of skills, of life partners, of potency, of intimacy, of privacy, and of familiar routines.

7. **Share The Pictures**

   Nothing is as powerful a trigger for the human memory as a photograph. Take the time to sit with the ones we love. Show them the pictures. Watch their eyes dance and come alive. The remote memory storage areas will be jump-started, and once again we will be blessed with another story revealing their soul.

8. **Hold Them Close**

This part is for you. There will come a time down the road when they and you won't be there to touch and hold. Do it now.

I hope this book provides strategies and solutions for you and your older loved ones. May your time together be a lasting legacy of love.

Jane Yousey

Section 1

Physical Well-Being and Aging

Chapter 1

How the Body Changes with Age

Imagine entering a room full of people at a party. Sounds like fun, right? Well, not so fast. The noise sounds like you're in a wind tunnel because your hearing device doesn't function optimally in noisy, open areas. You are told that "everyone you know will be there," but deep inside, you know that you can't remember their names. You can't even see well enough to watch them walking towards you, which might give you time to TRY to remember ... if you only could. And you can't remember for the moment who brought you here, so you feel some anxiety about when and how you are getting home. Sometimes ... it feels easier to just stay home.

Physical aging refers to the effects of aging on the body. Primary factors include heredity and genetics, while secondary factors include stress, disease, and injury. Many factors influence the aging process, including a person's:

- Physical environment
- Nutrition
- Medical care
- Stress
- Physical exercise
- Activity level
- Social Environment

Do you ever find yourself feeling impatient with an older person who talks constantly about his/her health? The truth is that aging brings changes in over ten systems in the body.

Muscular System

Older persons can experience a 10% decrease in strength between the ages of 30 and 60, mostly in the back and leg muscles. Muscles can lose their ability to expand and contract, which can limit movement. See that your older loved one exercises to maintain strength and flexibility. It is never too late to build strength.

Skeletal System

As a person ages, their bones decrease in mass, and are more susceptible to fracture. Decreased height and deteriorating posture are most often caused by atrophy of the discs between the vertebrae. Older persons may experience decreased flexibility in their spines, which can limit everyday movements. Bone density testing and calcium intervention can help, along with regular weight-bearing exercise.

Cardiovascular System

Many older persons experience a decrease in the heart's ability to respond to and recover from exertion. It takes patience on everyone's part to allow older folks the time to move more slowly.

Nervous System

Between the ages of 20 and 90, 30% of brain cells, called neurons, are lost. (We do lose our minds somewhat!) Changes in the a specific area of the brain called the hippocampus affect memory. You may see a decline in thinking speed and endurance.

Respiratory System

Changes in this system contribute to fatigue because it becomes more difficult to expel air from the lungs. Older persons may have a reduced ability to breathe deeply and cough.

Skin

Older skin tears more easily because it has become thinner. Wrinkles are caused by decreased muscle tone, decreased skin elasticity, and increased melatin. Hair loss is common. Do you hear complaints about your older loved ones feeling cold? This is because the skin no longer insulates as well. Atrophy of sweat and oil glands may also occur.

Metabolic System

The metabolic rate decreases with age. One theory of aging proposes that caloric restrictions after age 40 may prolong life. Smaller and more frequent meals are often more healthful. See Chapter Five, Nutrition and Meal Preparation Strategies for more information.

Endocrine System

Aging involves a decline in hormones associated with the immune system. This decreases the body's ability to protect itself, so illness occurs. As the body ages, it is increasingly affected by disease and illness and begins to wear out.

Urinary System

A decrease in renal blood flow can lead to an increase in waste products in the blood, along with kidney problems. Incomplete emptying of the bladder is common. In men, hypertrophy (or enlargement) of the prostate can cause leakage as pressure is felt on the urethra.

Gastrointestinal System

Smell and taste are diminished along with other senses, so food just doesn't seem to taste as good. The digestion process slows. Gastric enzymes like hydrochloric acid decrease, leading to incomplete breakdown of food and compromised nutrition.

Sensory System

One of the greatest changes that can occur as people age is a decline in the sensitivity of their vision, hearing, smell, taste, and touch.

Vision

Aging can cause weakening of the eye muscles, making it harder to focus on an image. Near vision is commonly affected. Cataracts, a clouding of the lens behind the pupil of the eye cause blurred and decreased vision and may require lens replacement. Macular degeneration affects the nerves in the retina and leads to loss of vision in the center of the visual field. Glaucoma arises when pressure inside the eyeball increases, damaging the optic nerve. If left untreated, glaucoma can cause tunnel vision.

Safety is the biggest concern with visual changes. Families and caregivers need to ensure that older persons can safely negotiate their way around their home and community, safely manage daily routines, and engage in activities that occupy their time in meaningful ways. Occupational therapists can assist by teaching techniques and adaptations for people with poor vision.

Some suggestions:
- Address persons by name so you have their attention.

- Sudden changes in light are more difficult for an older person to adjust to. When going inside or outside, allow time for their eyes to adjust to the new level of light.
- Do not rearrange furniture in an older person's room or home without walking through the new layout with them.
- Use an occupational therapist to evaluate home safety and recommend appropriate modifications.
- Ensure that there is adequate light for work areas and activities.
- Substitute large print labels and reading materials to assist an older person in being independent.
- Clearly mark and label medications in large print to ensure proper usage.

Hearing

By age 75, 40% of persons experience hearing loss; by age 85, this number has increased to 90%. Normal changes in hearing, especially in a person's ability to hear high frequencies, occur in just about everyone, but two more specific types of hearing loss may also occur. The first is conductive hearing loss, in which wax or fluid interferes with the way sound travels through the ear. More common in older persons is sensorineural hearing loss, which affects the way language is heard and understood.

Some suggestions:
- Speak more slowly and lower in tone, but do not shout.
- Make eye contact with the person to whom you are speaking, standing two to three feet in front of them.
- Eliminate distracting background noise such as music, fans, air conditioners, etc.

- Schedule regular check-ups with an audiologist as needed.
- Ensure that the lighting is adequate for the older person to see you as you speak.
- Alert the older person when changing subjects.
- Avoid covering your mouth or turning away as you speak.

Smell

Aging may bring a generalized decline in this sense, as the amount of mucous in the nose decreases. The sense of smell is critical to safety as this sense alerts the brain to the danger of fire, smoke, or noxious fumes. Smell is also an important component in nutrition, as inviting smells prompt a person to begin eating.

Some suggestions:
- Help an older person compensate for lack of smell by using visual signals to warn of danger: for example, alarms and blinking lights in the event of fire or smoke.
- Arrange food in an appetizing presentation, to encourage appetite when smell is impaired.

Taste

Many factors can affect an older person's sense of taste, including nerve damage and loss of mucous on the tongue. Often, dietary restrictions like reduced salt make food less tasty. When the consistency of food needs to be altered to alleviate the risk of choking, food looks less recognizable and smells less appetizing.

Some suggestions:
- Food needs to look appealing to taste good. Make every effort to arrange food in appropriate serving dishes.
- Avoid using bowls when inappropriate, or mixing food together.

- Instead of adding salt for flavor, use fresh herbs and spices that are both tasty and easily digested.

Touch

The awareness of various types of touch diminishes with age. Light touch is less recognizable, as is pain. Injury prevention is of the utmost importance with these changes, as an older person may not feel a break in the skin or an injured joint. Temperature sensitivity is also decreased, putting the older person at risk for hypothermia.

Some suggestions:
- Help older persons to inspect their bodies, especially their feet and limbs, for injury or abrasion each day.
- Encourage appropriate clothing and outerwear to prevent a drop in body temperature during cold weather.
- Body heat can quickly be lost through the hands, feet, and head; encourage older loved ones to wear gloves, boots, and hats as needed.
- Be alert for the safety of older persons in cold weather; they may get easily disoriented or confused.
- Other senses like vision and hearing can help an older person compensate for a decrease in the sense of touch.

C h a p t e r 2

Safety Concerns Inside the Home

A person's home is their castle, whether it is an apartment, a house, or an assisted living residence. It should be a place of rest, comfort, and safety. Unfortunately, 75% of falls occur at home. Of these falls, 50% are caused by environmental factors. Once a fall has occurred, an older person can experience a decline in overall health and a long, difficult recovery. Many times, an older person never regains the independence they had prior to the fall.

Steps can be taken to help prevent falls and ensure safety in the home. Listed below are ten easy adaptations that can be made to any home to reduce an older person's risk of falling. Occupational therapists can provide a much more thorough home evaluation and should be called on to maximize safety.

- **Remove throw rugs and secure carpet edges**
  It is extremely easy to catch a toe on the edge of a carpet that does not lie flat, or skid on a slippery throw rug. To solve these problems, apply double-sided tape to the edge of any loose carpeting. Purchase skid-resistant mats to place under throw rugs, or remove throw rugs entirely.

- **Evaluate lighting**

  Is the entryway properly illuminated? Are nightlights set to illuminate the path from the bedroom to the bath? Are light switches accessible in each room? Having to cross a darkened room to turn on a lamp is dangerous. Ensure switches are available at the entrance to each room, or consider the "clapper" switch to turn on lamps. Use automatic darkness detecting nightlights to illuminate the pathway from the bed to the bathroom. Be aware that glare from glossy floor surfaces can impede vision.

- **Double-rail all stairs**

  Adding a railing on both sides of a stairway increases the chances of recovery from a misstep or moment of imbalance. Make certain rails are securely attached to wall studs.

- **Install bathroom safety bars**

  Most falls occur in the bathroom where floors can be wet and slippery. Safety grab bars (not towel racks) should be installed in the tub/shower stall, as well as by the toilet. A plastic shower chair or tub bench allows the bather to sit rather than stand during a shower. Use a hand-held shower attachment in conjunction with the shower chair to avoid unnecessary standing.

- **Hide loose wires and extension cords**

  Any visible wire or cord can become a fall hazard. Tape down cords or tack them along the floor edge to minimize the risk of tripping. Hand-held portable phones eliminate dangerous telephone cords.

- **Eliminate clutter on floors**

  Scan the floor surface. Eliminate stacks of newspapers or magazines. Remove or reposition decorative items so they are not in the commonly used walking paths. Ensure that heating vents or radiators are clear of any flammable objects such as wicker baskets or magazine racks so that falls do not occur while trying to escape a dangerous emergency situation.

- **Use a rolling cart between the kitchen and dining room**

  Spills and burns are always a concern when transporting dishes to and from the kitchen. To help prevent accidents and reduce the risk of falls, use a small, rolling cart to transport hot plates and glasses. This cart is an ideal devise for anyone using a cane or walker.

- **Raise chair heights**

  An important fall consideration is how easy it is to get out of a seated position in the event of an emergency. The rule of thumb is that the lower the seat, the more energy it requires getting in and out of. By raising the height of a seat with an additional pillow or pad, less strain on the leg muscles is required and energy is conserved. The ideal seat is not a recliner, but rather a firm, stable armchair.

- **Simplify the entrance**

  Consider installing a keyless deadbolt lock to simplify entry into a home. Fumbling for keys can not only be frustrating, but also increases the risk of injury or danger. Falls can occur as an older person is rushing to avoid inclement weather, carrying packages, and trying to unlock the door with a key. An adapted door handle with keyless entry is also recommended for people with wrist pain due to arthritis.

- **Mark top and bottom steps**

  Aging can cause changes in how steps are perceived by an older person. To help prevent falls, mark the top and bottom steps with a different color paint or tape to distinguish them clearly from the floor.

Emergency Planning Checklist

Use this list to help your older loved ones organize important information in case of emergency. Create an emergency binder by placing information from this list in a three-ring binder that stays near their telephone directory. Certain emergency information should be carried in their wallet at all times. Update information as needed.

In Emergency Binder by Telephone:

____ List of medications and dosages.

____ List of emergency contact information, including names and phone numbers of doctors and family members.

____ Brief synopsis of health and medical history.

____ List of current health and life insurance policies.

____ List of military benefits.

____ Written copy of living will and directives.

____ List of bank account numbers.

____ List of financial records, including safety deposit boxes and accounts.

In Wallet:

____ List of emergency contact information, including names and phone numbers of doctors and family members.

____ Brief synopsis of health and medical history.

____ List of current health and life insurance policies.

____ List of medications and dosages.

C h a p t e r 3

Safety Issues Outside the Home

An older person's safety awareness and safety skill development is critical to successful aging. Feeling safe and trusting one's intuition gives an older person the confidence to maintain an active life outside the home. Many factors can affect a person's safety awareness and responsiveness, including:

- Fatigue and exhaustion.
- Acute illness
- Changes in mental wellness including stress, depression, or anxiety.
- Medication side effects including sedation or agitation.
- Challenging new environments and unfamiliar locations.
- Normal changes due to aging such as decreased hearing and vision.

Older persons can put themselves at risk by not paying close attention to their physical surroundings and the people around them. Developing keen safety awareness can help an older person from injuring himself or herself.

Safety Checklist

The checklist below can be used to review safety awareness with older persons.

Body Language

___ Regularly scan your surroundings to communicate alertness and watchfulness.

___ Be aware of who is behind you and beside you at all times.

___ Walk with a companion if possible.

___ Be able to describe where you are at all times.

___ Use your sense of intuition and instinct to sense danger.

Street Safety

___ Keep valuables like jewelry hidden under outer garments.

___ Avoid being weighed down with packages and bags. Keep your hands free.

___ Keep your wallet or purse hidden as much as possible.

___ Wear a purse across the body, not on one shoulder.

___ Look around as you walk, watching for anything out of the ordinary that could cause concern.

___ Walk with a sense of confidence.

___ Do not speak to people unfamiliar to you.

___ Do not carry your keys in your hand.

Emergency Preparedness

___ Keep a list of current medications with you in your wallet.

___ Carry a telephone calling card with you for emergency phone calls.

___ Keep a list of persons to contact in case of emergency, including your physician's name and phone number.

____   Wear a bracelet to alert others to any medical conditions such as diabetes.

____   Be ready to shout or move quickly if in sudden danger.

Walking Safety

____   Carry a portable phone in case of emergency.

____   Wear reflective clothing for late afternoon walks.

____   Wear comfortable, loose-fitting clothing in layers you can shed if you feel warm.

____   Vary your walking route so that you cannot easily be followed.

____   Walk in well-traveled areas with lots of people around.

____   Be aware of high-risk areas in the community or neighborhood.

____   Wear comfortable, rubber-soled shoes for good traction.

____   Walk inside a mall during inclement weather.

____   Be aware of safe places to take sitting breaks when out walking.

____   Have a walking partner.

____   Walk on a populated fitness trail or track safe from motor traffic.

C h a p t e r 4

Exercise Strategies for Successful Aging

What does it mean to be fit in later life? What are the benefits of adding regular exercise to a daily routine? Is it too late to turn around life-long patterns of inactivity? What precautions should be taken before beginning an exercise program?

Older persons face many challenges in accomplishing important daily tasks. Body movements that came easily in younger years can now prove difficult. Daily tasks such as reaching high shelves, climbing a flight of stairs, or bending to reach items on the floor, as well as household chores like mopping or vacuuming, carrying grocery bags, or simply making a bed, require flexibility, endurance, and strength.

In addition to assisting daily functioning, exercise has been shown to reduce the risk of developing diabetes, high blood pressure, heart disease, osteoporosis, and some forms of cancer.

Regular physical activity has been shown to:
- Improve mood and energy levels.
  After just ten minutes of increased heart rate, study participants at Northern Arizona University showed improved overall mood and energy levels.
- Strengthen bones and build muscle.

Exercise is an important defense against osteoporosis.

- Improve the control of diabetes by lowering blood sugar levels, and help protect against heart disease.
- Strengthen the cardiovascular system by improving circulation, helping people better manage weight, blood pressure, and cholesterol levels.
- Improve functioning for persons with arthritis by helping to reduce swelling in joints.
- Improve a person's sense of control and self-esteem. Researchers at Washington University School of Medicine found that even frail, elderly people benefit from increasing their level of physical activity. Looking at 1733 people whose average age was 73, researchers found improved emotional health with increased physical activity.

Getting Started

When helping an older person decide what exercise program might be appropriate, keep the following guidelines in mind:

- Before beginning any exercise program, consult a physician for limitations, and precautions.
- Set clear, measurable goals with the help of an exercise physiologist, occupational therapist, or physical therapist.
- Exercise programs help to maintain function, flexibility, and strength, while helping to prevent injury. Different persons will benefit in different ways.
- Wear comfortable, non-restrictive clothing and appropriate footwear.
- Choose an exercise program or activity that is interesting and feels good.
- Start slowly and make gradual but steady gains.
- Get plenty of sleep and proper nutrition for a well-balanced life.

Helping Your Loved One Set Goals

The Surgeon General's Office recommends 30 minutes of physical activity a day; this can be broken down into small time periods and accumulated over the day. Seniors should exercise at least three to five times per week, based on physicians' recommendations for injury prevention. According to the President's Council on Physical Fitness, the amount and type of physical activity will vary according to a person's goals.

Health or Fitness Goal	Activities to Include in Fitness Program
Getting started	Daily physical activity, such as walking, stretching, or active movement, for 30 minutes or more.
Improved flexibility	Daily stretching of each area of the body, holding the stretch for 15 seconds and repeating 3 times.
Improved overall strength	Combination of a daily walk or swim with resistance exercises for each area of the body.
Cardiovascular fitness	Vigorous activity for 30 minutes, 3 to 5 times per week.
Weight Management	Balance of food intake and daily activity to insure that recommended weight is maintained .
Endurance and strength	Cardiovascular activity, along with weight-bearing exercises, 3 times per week.

Each exercise session should include a period of:
- Warm-up.
- Conditioning.
- Cool-down.

Warm-Up
Any exercise session should begin with a period of easy muscle stretching and deep breathing, because warm muscles will stretch more easily than cold muscles, stretching is most effective after a five to ten-minute period of easy walking.

Conditioning
The conditioning phase of the exercise session helps the body's circulatory and respiratory systems. The heart and lungs are conditioned with low-impact, large muscle movements such as walking, bike riding, or swimming. This phase also includes strengthening, resistance, and weight-bearing exercises.

Cool-Down
Movements slow down during this phase. Stretching is important to maintain flexibility.

Balance for Life
Balance and fall prevention are a major concern for older persons. Please refer to chapter 2 for details on safety for older persons.

For More Information:

American Diabetes Association
  www.diabetes.org

National Osteoporosis Foundation
  www.nof.org/prevention/exercise.htm

American Heart Association
  www.justmove.org/home.cfm

Agency for Healthcare Research and Quality
  www.ahrq.gov

American Council on Exercise
  www.acefitness.org

American Association of Retired Persons
  www.aarp.com

Novartis Foundation for Gerontology
  www.healthandage.com

Exercise Check List

Before beginning any exercise program, consult a physician for limitations, precautions, and physical restrictions. Stop exercise immediately and consult a physician if any of the following occur during exercise:

____ Racing or slow pulse
____ Fatigue
____ Breathlessness
____ Disorientation
____ Confusion
____ Dizziness
____ Lightheaded feeling
____ Decreased coordination
____ Numbness or tingling in hands or feet
____ Discomfort
____ Inability to carry on a conversation
____ Change in skin color: either pale or flushed
____ Sudden pain

Chapter 5

Nutrition and Meal Preparation Strategies

Good nutrition for seniors can help maintain energy levels, prevent disease, maintain the strength necessary for mobility, and improve functioning in daily activities.

Many factors can affect an older person's nutrition status, including appetite, changes in taste buds, medication, difficulty in meal preparation/shopping, inability to afford a well-balanced diet, decreased mental ability, medical conditions, difficulty chewing and swallowing, and lack of energy to prepare meals. When concerns arise that an older person is not getting proper nutrition, a professional dietitian should be consulted.

Diseases that are affected by nutrition include heart disease, diabetes, obesity, tooth loss, osteoporosis, stroke, and degenerative arthritis.

Nutrition and Aging

Most seniors need fewer calories than they did when they were younger. This happens for two reasons. First, most seniors are not as active physically as they once were, and therefore require fewer calories. Secondly, the amount of energy needed to maintain normal body functions like heart rate and breathing decreases with age. A person's need for vitamins and minerals does not decrease, however. Many older persons experience a decrease in appetite as they age; eating frequent smaller meals instead of three large ones per day may help.

The aging process causes physical changes that may affect nutrition and digestion. These include:

Area of Change	Recommendations and Suggestions
Chewing and Swallowing	• Dental pain can interfere with proper nutrition. Use a soft diet as needed until dental problems are resolved. • Consult an occupational therapist for a complete swallowing evaluation.
Concentration	• Eliminate distracting background noise. • Turn off radio and television.
Dry mouth	• Alternate bites with sips of a beverage. • Use gravy or sauces to moisten food. • Dunk dry foods in coffee or tea.
Decreased sense of taste	• Make foods more appealing by using flavorful seasonings like onion, garlic, and fresh herbs. • Garnish foods with colorful vegetables. • Marinate meats in dressing, fruit juice, or wine to enhance flavor. • Use lemon and herbs to make vegetables more zesty.
Constipation	• Eat a high-fiber diet. • Drink plenty of fluids.

Food Guide Pyramid

The US Department of Agriculture and the Department of Health and Human Services have created a Food Guide Pyramid to assist with daily food choices. The recommendations include:

- 6-11 servings per day from the bread, rice, cereal, and pasta group.
- 3-5 servings per day from the vegetable group.
- 2-4 servings from the fruit group.
- 2-3 servings from the milk, yogurt, and cheese group.
- 2-3 servings from the meat, poultry, fish, dry beans, eggs, and nuts group.
- Use fats, oils, and sweets sparingly.

Affording Nutritious Food

Suggestions for seniors include:

1. Use store and manufacturer's discount coupons if possible.
2. Don't shop on an empty stomach.
3. Look for Senior Discount Days.
4. Prepare a list for grocery shopping based on healthful, well-balanced meals.
5. Avoid spontaneous purchases.
6. Read labels to determine what products are the most nutritious for the money.
7. Avoid purchasing high-sugar, high-fat products.
8. Buy foods that are both healthful and easy to prepare.
9. Avoid restaurant and fast-food meals.
10. Prepare home made TV dinners and freeze until needed.

Planning Healthy and Easy Meals

The American Association of Retired Persons (AARP) has developed a list of foods that can be prepared quickly and easily:

• Prepared tomato sauce • Canned beans for salads, soups, and casseroles • Fresh, canned, and frozen vegetables • Fresh, canned, and frozen fruit • Low-fat cottage cheese • Low-fat yogurt	• Whole-grain breads • High-fiber cereals • Canned tuna, chicken, or salmon • Low-fat/low-sodium chicken or beef broth • Boneless chicken breasts • Flour tortillas • Pita bread

Nutrition to Fight Disease

The Nutrition Action Newsletter (April 1996) highlights five foods that are especially healthful for seniors.

1. **Calcium-Fortified Orange Juice**
   The additional calcium makes this the most healthful juice one can drink. Incorporate it into your diet as part of the recommended daily servings of fruit.

2. **Canned Salmon or Sardines**
   The fish oil, calcium, protein, and vitamin C make this a super food for seniors. Be careful to combine this salty food with lower sodium complements.

3. **Whole-Grain / High Fiber Cold Cereal**
   This low-fat food helps prevent constipation and may lower the risk of colon cancer.

4. **Collard Greens, Kale, and Spinach**
   High in lutein, these greens may reduce the risk of macular degeneration, the leading cause of blindness among older persons.

5. **Skim Milk**
   High in protein, low in fat, and a great source of calcium!

Water for Health

Many seniors do not drink enough water due to a fear of incontinence. Not only is this dangerous, it decreases an older person's ability to function at peak levels.

- 75% of Americans are chronically dehydrated. (This likely applies to half of the world's population.)
- In 37% of Americans, the thirst mechanism is so weak that it is often mistaken for hunger.
- Even mild dehydration will slow down one's metabolism as much as 3%.
- One glass of water was shown to stop midnight hunger pangs for almost 100% of the dieters studied in a recent university study.
- Dehydration is the number one trigger of daytime fatigue.
- Preliminary research indicates that 8 to10 glasses of water a day could significantly ease back and joint pain for up to 80% of sufferers.
- A mere 2% drop in hydration can trigger fuzzy short-term memory, trouble with basic math, and difficulty focusing on a computer screen or on a printed page.
- Drinking 5 glasses of water daily decreases the risk of colon cancer by 45%, it can slash the risk of breast cancer by 79%, and one is 50% less likely to develop bladder cancer.

Food and Medication Interaction
Some food and medication combinations keep important nutrients from being absorbed by the body, or interfere with how the medication should work.

1. Make certain that the doctor knows all the prescriptions and over-the-counter medications a patient is taking.
2. Ask the pharmacist or doctor how medications may interact with foods.
3. Report any unusual side effects or symptoms with any medication.
4. Take medications as prescribed, noting warnings about drug interactions with alcohol or certain foods.
5. Read package labels and inserts carefully.

Services to Enhance Good Nutrition

When cooking and/or shopping are no longer possible for an older loved one, consider the following options:

1. Ask local food stores to deliver groceries. Some charge; others do not.
2. Consider Meals-on-Wheels for a hot, midday meal.
3. Ask a church or synagogue for volunteer help.
4. Investigate what meals are served at the local senior center.
5. Hire a home health worker to shop and prepare meals at home.
6. Consider a living environment that provides at least one meal per day.

Nutrition Resources

New England Journal of Medicine
    content.nejm.org

USDA Food and Nutrition Information Center
    www.nal.usda.gov/fnic/

USDA Index of Food and Nutrition Internet Resources
    www.nal.usda.gov/fnic/fnic-etexts.html

American Heart Association
    Infoline: 1-800-242-8721
    www.amhrt.org

American Dietetic Association
    Nutrition Hotline: 1-800-366-1655
    www.eatright.org

National Cholesterol Education Program
    National Heart, Lung, & Blood Institute
    Infoline: 1-800-575-WELL
    www.nhlbi.nih.gov/nhlbi/nhlbi.htm

Council for Responsible Nutrition
  1300 19th St., N.W., Suite 310
  Washington, D.C. 20036
  Information: 1-202-872-1488
  www.social.com/health/nhic/data/hr0000/hr0090.html

Department of Agriculture
  U.S. Department of Agriculture
  Center for Nutrition Policy and Promotion
  14th and Independence Ave, S.W., Suite 240-E
  Washington, D.C. 20250
  www.usda.gov

National Cancer Institute
  Cancer Information Service: 1-800-422-6237
  www.nci.nih.gov

American Institute of Cancer Research
  Nutrition Hotline: 1-800-843-8114
  www.AICR.org

Brigham and Women's Hospital, Harvard Medical School
  www.med.harvard.edu/BWHRad/

Institute of Food Technologies
  221 N. LaSalle St., Ste. 300
  Chicago, IL 60601-1291
  Telephone: 312-782-8424
  Fax: 312-782-8348
  www.ift.org

Nutritional Check List

Here is a list of nutritional recommendations. Consult a dietitian or physician for proper nutritional guidelines for your older loved one.

____ Drink 8 glasses of water daily.

____ Eat 6 to 9 servings of fruit and vegetables per day.

____ Eat a low-fat diet with 2 to 4 servings of protein per day.

____ Take in 1000 to 1500 mg of calcium per day, either from low-fat foods or with a supplement.

____ Eat at least 3 meals per day.

____ Maintain appropriate doctor-recommended weight.

____ Alert your physician to any unintentional 10-pound weight gain or loss.

____ Limit caffeine intake.

____ Limit alcohol intake to less than 2 drinks per day.

____ Limit fast food intake to once per week.

____ Get regular dental exams. Wear proper fitting dentures as needed.

____ Eat slowly and without distractions. Sit upright at a table.

____ Plan meals in advance.

____ Read food labels and get help in understanding what the label means.

____ Take a multivitamin that supplies 100% of the USDA's recommended daily intake of most vitamins and minerals.

____ Avoid between-meal snacks.

Chapter 6

Driving Safety For Seniors

Many families struggle with the thought of discussing driving safety with older loved ones because of the emotional reaction they expect. For many seniors, the ability to drive represents freedom and independence. This desire for freedom is at times more powerful than the desire to be safe.

Changes brought on by aging can frequently be seen in a person's reflex speed and reaction time. This is due to a decrease in both the number of neurons in the nervous system and the speed at which they function. In the older person, this results in decreased coordination, decreased reaction time, and increased difficulty in maintaining balance. Changes in vision and hearing, including impaired depth perception, misjudged distances, and decreased visual field, contribute to driving difficulties. Medications can affect a person's driving safety, as can changes in mental functioning and safety awareness.

General Driving Safety for Seniors:
- Always wear a shoulder and lap seat belt.
- Keep car doors locked at all times.
- Keep a list of emergency phone numbers and contacts in the glove box.
- Keep a flare in the car to signal in case of emergency.
- Never, under any circumstances, stop to pick up a stranger.

- Keep the car in optimal working order, including regular tire rotation and oil changes.
- Avoid riding as a passenger in a car with an unsafe driver. It is better to risk hurt feelings than to risk your life.
- Make certain that the windshield is clean and the wipers are working effectively.
- Occasionally clean the headlights to increase illumination.

Ways to Increase Driving Comfort:
- Push the car seat as far back as possible before getting into the car.
- Back into the seat, sit down when the seat is against the back of your legs, and gently swing one leg in at a time.
- Pull the seat forward once you are comfortably seated in the car.
- Use an inflatable air seat cushion to absorb bumps on the road.

Steps to Assess Driving Safety:
1. Begin with the driving self-assessment to help older persons assess their own driving safety and ability.
1. Review current medications with older persons, noting warning labels about operating motor vehicles.
2. Assist the older person in scheduling annual exams with an eye care professional to measure visual acuity.
3. Suggest a driver refresher course.
   - "Safe Driving for Mature Operators" is offered by AAA. Contact your local American Automobile Association club.
   - "55 Alive / Mature Driving" is offered by AARP and is very affordable. Call 1-800-424-3410 to register.
   - "Coaching the Mature Driver" is offered by the US National Safety Council. Call 1-800-621-7619 for more information.

4. Help ensure proper body positioning in the car by adding adaptations such as higher seat cushions or enlarged side mirrors.

5. If night-time vision is difficult, avoid driving at night. If rush hour traffic increases anxiety and stress, travel during alternate times.

6. Drive back roads to avoid the speed of highways and superhighways.

7. Use a professional service, like an occupational therapist specializing in driver evaluation, to help determine driving safety and reaction time.

8. If driving is clearly dangerous for the older person, it is time for a frank discussion. Prepare by doing your research for your loved ones: suggest possible solutions like senior community transportation services, to help maintain as much independence as possible.

Driving Safety Check List

Assess a person's driving safety by having them answer the following questions:

___ Are you having any difficulty judging distances, such as when pulling into a parking space between two cars?

___ Have you had any minor "fender benders" in the past year?

___ Have you had any near-misses recently?

___ Do other drivers beep, glare, or signal at you?

___ Do you find yourself driving slower than most traffic on the road?

___ Do you feel especially anxious while you are driving?

___ Do cars suddenly seem to appear in your vision without warning?

___ Do you depend on others in the car to help you see or judge distances?

___ Is driving at night-time more difficult for you?

___ Are others concerned about your driving?

Chapter 7

Saving Energy by Working Smarter, Not Harder

The time comes in life when using your head makes more sense than using your muscles. Working smarter, not harder, makes good sense at any age, but pays off especially during the senior years. When older persons are able to conserve their energy during chores and household tasks, they have more energy for recreation, socialization, and leisure.

Use the following suggestions to help older loved ones work smarter, not harder.

Body Posture and Positioning Guidelines
- Avoid heavy lifting. When carrying lighter items, hold them close to the body.
- Avoid twisting or turning when carrying items or when bending: this puts too much strain on the lower back.
- Be aware of your posture. Keep your head upright, tummy tucked in, and allow your legs to do the work.
- Sit down as much as possible when doing a repeated task for a long period of time, such as ironing, folding clothes, or chopping food.

Dressing
- Hang items by outfit instead of individually. Put a blouse and matching skirt on the same hanger, or pants and a matching shirt. Then, reach into the closet only once to dress each morning.
- Put on blouse, socks, and shirt from a seated position. Have an armchair easily accessible near the closet.
- Keep undergarments in a top drawer to avoid bending.
- Use loops on the backs of slippers to help pull them on easily.

Kitchen Work
- Instead of carrying heavy items like juice and milk, slide them along the counter surface between the refrigerator and the food preparation area or sink.
- Save yourself miles of steps by mentally making the list of items needed from the refrigerator and getting them all out at once.
- Use a rolling cart to transport items in one trip. On this cart, place all utensils, napkins, and dishes for the table setting.
- Use electrical appliances, such as an electric knife, a mixer, and an electric can opener, to simplify work.
- To avoid bending, use a countertop toaster/broiler/ oven instead of a large, conventional oven.
- Buy cooking utensils with large foam handles to reduce the amount of strain on hand/finger joints.

Shopping
- When bagging, create smaller, lighter loads instead of fewer, heavier bags
- Have groceries delivered whenever possible.
- Make lists and organize your shopping route based on the store's layout. Ask for assistance when having to reach or bend for heavy items.
- Many stores provide electric carts for customer use; take advantage of these as needed.

Laundry

- Use a rolling laundry hamper with handles. Avoid large, heavy loads by washing more frequently.
- Use separate hampers for light and dark loads to avoid the step of sorting laundry.
- Use concentrated detergents that come in smaller, lighter soap bottles.
- Use spray stain removers instead of scrubbing.
- Use top-loading machines to avoid bending and strain. If necessary, raise a front-loading machine to a more convenient height by placing it on a platform.
- Remove clothes from the dryer immediately to avoid unnecessary ironing. Hang or fold in the same step.
- Use an adjustable ironing board to do the ironing in a seated position.

Making the Bed

- Use the "once around the bed" rule. Smooth sheets and blankets while still in the bed, then make final adjustments to covers when out of the bed.
- Use elastic-cornered fitted sheets or sheet clamps to secure corners, to avoid having to smooth every day.
- Avoid heavy quilts and covers if experiencing foot pain. Use a down-filled coverlet for lightweight warmth.

Cleaning

- Use a daily tub/shower spray for bathtubs and shower stalls.
- Purchase long-handled brooms, dust pans, and mops to avoid bending.
- Place waste cans in every room.
- Transport cleaning supplies in a rolling cart. Keep a set of cleaning supplies on every level of your house.
- Wear a cleaning apron with pockets for sponges, towels, dust cloths, and small items that are picked up along the way.
- Dust from a seated position using a dust cloth in each hand.

Cooking and Meal Preparation

- Gather all ingredients on the counter before beginning the recipe.
- Use a bar stool or kitchen stool to sit on while working.
- Use microwave or oven cooking instead of stove-top cooking to avoid long periods of standing over the stove.
- Cook double quantities and freeze the second meal for reheating another time.
- Keep tools and equipment stored near the preparation area to avoid continually crossing the kitchen work area.
- Serve meals in cooking containers to eliminate double clean-up.
- Soak cooking containers in hot, soapy water to soften for easy clean-up.

General Storage Hints

- Store frequently used items at a comfortable height, generally between waist and shoulder height.
- Use the highest and lowest shelves for infrequently used items like seasonal storage.
- Pull-out shelves like those on rollers or bearings make items stored in the back of a cabinet more accessible.
- Store items near the point of use, like potholders next to the oven and pot covers near the stove.
- Commonly used electrical appliances like coffeemakers should be stored on the countertop near accessible outlets.
- Eliminate clutter in drawers and cabinets.

Leisure and Relaxation

- Sit in a chair with a supportive back and a footrest to elevate feet.
- Make getting in and out of a chair easier by sliding forward to the edge of the chair, then pushing against both arm rests, bending forward to align nose over toes.

- The higher the seat, the less strain there will be on leg muscles when sitting or standing.
- Ensure adequate lighting for activities.
- Use a book rest to eliminate the need for holding up a book while reading.

Chapter 8

Managing Pain Successfully

Everyone experiences pain at some time in life. Pain is the number one reason older persons seek medical attention. Over 80% of people will experience lower back pain during their lifetime, and 50% of people will experience neck pain. Pain is often very difficult to describe, and the measure of pain is perceived differently by each person.

Pain is actually the body's message to stop a potentially dangerous activity that may cause tissue damage, or to escape a dangerous event. Pain, however, can continue far beyond the time when the danger source is removed. At this point, pain no longer is productive and can become quite disabling.

Acute pain usually occurs with an injury or sudden damage to the body, and lasts less than three months. Damage can occur to bones, muscles, ligaments, tendons, and joints, as well as nerve tissue. Pain can result from many things including overuse, inflammation, infection, fracture, and dislocation. Acute pain is commonly treated through rest, use of cold or heat packs (determined by a medical professional), and analgesic and/or anti-inflammatory medications. It is critical that acute pain be addressed properly, to prevent its turning into chronic pain.

Chronic pain includes a complicated set of characteristics that can be extremely frustrating to both patients and caregivers. Chronic pain has not only a physical aspect to it, but a psychological one as well. This type of pain can occur in conjunction with a long-term physical condition (such as arthritis), or when the recovery period from an injury has gone on much longer than expected. Chronic pain management addresses three areas: the physical impact, the social impact, and the psychological impact. All three areas of impact need to be addressed in treatment.

Treatment for the Physical Impact of Pain may include:
- Medications to manage pain.
- Medications to stabilize sleep patterns.
- Modalities such as heat packs, whirlpools, ice packs, and transcutaneous electrical nerve stimulation (TENS) can often be effective.
- Nerve blocks, surgical treatment, trigger point injections, acupuncture, and mobilization may also be recommended.
- Critical to a person's function is the ability to perform daily activities as independently as possible. This may take strength or flexibility training, the use of adaptive equipment, and the appropriate environmental set-up to ensure success. Occupational therapists provide all these services in both the home and rehabilitation setting.
- Pain charting and journaling help identify patterns in a person's pain experience. Noted are time and location of pain, what makes it worse or better, description of pain (often in the form of a number scale), and information as to whether the pain travels or radiates.
- Alternative pain management techniques such as relaxation tools

Treatment for Social Factors may include:
- Marital education and support to help spouses understand how they can be most supportive to

someone with chronic pain, yet not feed into dysfunctional relationship behaviors.

- Support for family, friends, and spouse to help deal with the frustration and anger they may be experiencing.
- Family education and support to address how to best break chronic pain patterns that are detrimental to all members of the family.
- Treatment in a group or individual setting to address communication about pain, feedback about behaviors that push people away, and behavior modification techniques.
- Support from others who are managing chronic pain, and overcoming pain-related limitations.
- Discussion of issues related to self-concept, self-perception, and self-esteem

Treatment for Psychological Factors may include:
- Stress management and instruction on how to deal more effectively with the daily challenges of chronic pain.
- Relaxation training to reduce the perception of pain and better manage stress.
- Grief support to help deal with losses such as life roles, physical abilities, meaningful activities, independence, and previous life dreams and goals.
- Screening for changes in mood, social interaction, appetite, energy, and sleep that may indicate depression.
- Biofeedback can offer a person immediate information as to what they are doing to cause increased tension, anxiety, muscle tightening, and a change in skin temperature. Helping a person to relax using biofeedback may decrease the pain experience and improve restful sleep.

Treatment may include a combination of approaches that will decrease a person's pain experience, and at the same time, work to increase a person's ability to reengage in meaningful daily activities, relationships, and responsibilities. A person's motivation is critical to their management of pain. Occasionally, a person may fear that if they get better or no longer complain about their pain, they will be ignored, or perhaps will be forced to take back responsibilities they no longer want. These are called secondary gains to being in pain, and should be addressed by professionals familiar with pain management such as physicians, nurses, social workers, occupational therapists and physical therapists.

Common False Beliefs Regarding Pain and the Older Person
- Pain is part of growing older.
  Wrong! Unfortunately, older folks may not be willing to talk about their pain because they believe it shows weakness, or they may fear the treatment. Some people may not be able to express their pain in words, while others believe that it is courageous to "grin and bear it. "
- People become more sensitive to pain as they age.
  This is not necessarily true. With decreased sensitivity or changes in mental functioning, older folks can actually become *less* aware of pain. Look for changes in behavior like agitation and pacing.
- If a person does not complain of pain, then they don't have it.
  Wrong! There may be underlying fears preventing them from complaining. Perhaps they believe that pain is part of the normal aging experience. Perhaps they fear that something life-threatening has gone undiagnosed, and they don't want to know about it.
- A person who sleeps well must not be feeling pain.
  Pain is actually exhausting to the body, mind, and spirit. Excessive sleep can be indicative of underlying depression.

Chronic Pain Check List

Listed below are some common characteristics of chronic pain. Consult a doctor is you notice that:

_____ Pain has lasted more than 3 months.

_____ Pain causes a limitation in daily routines and activities.

_____ Pain is accompanied by either a chronic illness or persistent symptoms from an injury that should have resolved itself.

_____ Pain has not been resolved with the recommended course of medical intervention and therapy.

_____ Pain has affected key relationships for the individual, including family and friends.

_____ Pain has been addressed through multiple courses of medication and medical services.

_____ Surgeries and treatments have not proven effective.

_____ Considerable daily communication by the person refers to their level of pain, limitations, and treatments.

_____ Depressive symptoms, including social withdrawal, sad mood, and sleep or appetite disturbance may be noted.

_____ Much of the day is spent in bed, on the sofa, or in a reclining position.

Chapter 9

Medication Strategies

Older prsons may fear taking medications. Some seniors have experienced uncomfortable or undesirable side effects from previous prescriptions, while others fear being overly sedated and losing control of some of their bodily functions. Some seniors believe that taking medications early in the pain cycle may lessen their effectiveness later, when they are really needed. Addiction is frequently an underlying fear for the older person. Partnering with a doctor who is willing to streamline the number of medications and at the same time educate patients about possible adverse side effects will help alleviate fears.

Medication Compliance

Many factors affect medication compliance. If your older loved one is missing dosages, then the following possible reasons need to be explored with them:

- Could they be experiencing increased confusion for a variety of reasons including urinary tract infection or medication error?
- Is vision a factor – not being able to read the medicine bottle label?
- Is the medication packaging too difficult for them to open?

- Are financial limitations inhibiting the proper administration of medications?
- Could they be losing sensation in their fingers and as a result be dropping pills?

Communication Tips When Discussing Medications with Older Loved Ones

1. Talk in understandable and consistent terms
   Medication discussions can be complicated, so keep your language as simple as possible. Use the term "medication" consistently and avoid using the terms "drugs" or "pills."

2. Use eye contact
   Eye contact is a valuable communication tool to gauge whether someone is listening and understanding you.

3. Introduce the topic
   Start with a simple prompt like, "Mom, could we take a minute and talk about your medications?" This gives the older person awareness of the topic of discussion and time to gather thoughts and questions. Follow-up with written instructions or a schedule as needed.

4. Avoid distractions
   Communication is often misunderstood when background activity causes distraction.

5. Keep the discussion specific and clear
   Use specific times like 7am, 4pm, etc., instead of "twice a day."

Are medications being taken as prescribed?

HOW medications are taken is very important. Help your older loved one clearly understand the doctor's instructions. Should the medications be taken on a fixed schedule or as needed? Should the medications be taken on a full or an empty stomach? Are there any foods that would interfere with the medication's effectiveness? Should alcoholic beverages be eliminated? Will the medications affect your loved one's ability to drive safely?

Medication Reminder Systems

Many options exist to help seniors maintain the proper schedule for medication. Local home health organizations can assist seniors and their families in choosing the right reminder system. Options include:

- A pager system where an alarm sounds when it is medication time. This can be used at home or in the community.
- An alarm-clock system that can sound several times a day.
- An answering service that telephones the older person when it is medication time.
- A locked medication box, which not only sounds an alarm, but also automatically opens a drawer that has been pre-filled with the correct dosage. All other drawers, with other dosages, remain locked.
- Medication checklists containing medication names (both brand names and generic), dosage times, dosage amounts, and dosage frequency, along with how the medication is to be taken (with milk, etc.)
- Persons whose responsibility it is to stop by the home and administer medications as prescribed.

Adverse Drug Reaction Check List

Do not assume that changes in behavior are part of the "normal" aging process. Consider prescribed medications as well as over-the-counter medications as possible contributing factors. Consider the length of time your older loved one has been taking a particular medication, and understand that adverse reactions can happen at any time and on any dosage level.

Use this checklist to help assess adverse drug reactions. Contact your doctor and pharmacist if you notice any of the following symptoms or behaviors:

____ New involuntary movements.

____ Unusual mouth movements, especially in the tongue and lips.

____ Agitation and restlessness.

____ Unexplained dizziness, lightheadedness, or weakness.

____ Unusual posture such as arched back.

____ Shuffling walking pattern.

____ Tremors or shaking in arms or legs.

____ Changes in appetite.

____ Presence of nausea, vomiting, or diarrhea.

____ Confusion or disorientation.

____ Blurred vision.

____ Ringing in the ears.

____ Skin rash or irritation.

____ Loss of balance or instability.

____ Lethargy, drowsiness, or sedation.

____ Dark stools or discolored urine.

____ Changes in heart rate, breathing, or pulse.

Chapter *10*

Professional Programs and Services For Seniors

Seniors frequently express their concern about how hard it is to get older. Many factors contribute to these feelings. One strong, commonly held fear is that as a person ages, he or she may not be able to live independently. Statistics actually contradict this. Studies show that Americans are not only living longer, but also more independently. The August 2001 Life Extension Magazine had the following statistics:

> In 1982, 6.2% of the nation's elderly were confined to nursing homes, compared with only 3.4% in 1999. While there are nearly a third more elderly Americans in 1999 than in 1982, the total number of chronically disabled older Americans actually dropped.

From 1990 to 2000, the United States Census Bureau reported a 38% jump in the number of Americans over the age of 85. Given these changing patterns in aging, more and more seniors are able to live well in their homes with just a bit of support and assistance.

Finding out what services are available to seniors is often overwhelming. Start with a municipal employee who knows what the community offers. In some cases, families might consider paying for the services of a case management agency to identify, arrange, and monitor services for seniors.

Services to Support the Healthy Older Person

- **Community Senior Centers** offer a variety of programs, ranging from daily hot lunches to educational classes to social activities and trips. Many offer some kind of door-to-door transportation program as well.
- **Community Clubs and Organizations** offer outreach programs for seniors, senior expos, and specialty events to help meet the changing needs of seniors. These organizations are also a wonderful place for seniors to contribute their many gifts and skills as volunteers.
- **YMCA** programs offer specialized fitness activities for seniors.
- **Occupational Therapists** provide home evaluations to maximize safety and reduce the risk of falls in the home and community.
- **Malls and Shopping Centers** are providing structured walking programs on their premises to offer a safe, well-lit environment for daily walks. Contact the mall management office for details.
- **Churches and Religious Centers** offer free programs for seniors including thrift shops, hot meals, social events, transportation to help seniors attend worship services, and visitation programs.
- **Cable Television Shows,** such as Life Talk for Seniors in Connecticut, offer a wide range of programming to support seniors living in the community.
- **Financial Management Programs** offered by area Agencies on Aging can provide volunteers to help a senior balance a checkbook, write checks, organize a budget, etc.
- **Caregiver Support Groups** are common in most metropolitan areas, and provide tools and techniques to help meet the needs of caregivers.
- **Senior Support Groups** are offered through most local community mental health clinics to assist seniors with transitioning, anxiety, and depression.

Services to Support the Older Person with Impairments

- **Adult Day Care** programs listed in the Yellow Pages offer a safe, structured environment, along with social activities, to help seniors with impairments remain active. Most of these programs run for an eight-hour day, one to five days per week. Insurance usually does not cover the cost of such services.

- **Home Delivered Meals** for homebound persons can be arranged through Meals on Wheels. Local, state, and federal programs contribute to home delivered meal services. Sometimes a small fee or voluntary donation is requested.

- **Retired Senior Volunteer Services (RSVP)** offers volunteers to visit or phone homebound seniors, keeping seniors both connected to the community as well as monitored for their well-being.

- **Senior Housing Developments** sometimes offer semi-independent living, providing one hot meal at midday in a common dining area as well as a wide range of social and recreational activities.

- **Transportation** to medical appointments is sometimes available through organizations like the American Red Cross, the American Cancer Society, or Community Senior Service Programs.

- **Home Health Services** are paid for both privately and by insurance companies with a physician's referral, and can include a variety of professional services including:
  - ✦ **Nursing** to manage medications and medical issues.
  - ✦ **Therapy** including occupational, physical, and speech to help restore a person to a prior level of functioning.
  - ✦ **Social Work** to assist with family dynamics, mental health, planning, and support issues.
  - ✦ **Home Health Aid** to assist with self-care, hygiene, and grooming.

✧ **Homemaker** services are non-medical personnel who assist with shopping, cooking, light cleaning, companionship, and laundry.

✧ **Companions** provide assistance when persons cannot be left alone or desire socialization. These can vary from a few hours per week to full-time live-in status, paid privately.

Checklist of Helpful Organizations for Senior Services

____ Visiting Nurse Association of America (800) 426-2547

____ National Institute of Senior Centers (202) 479-1200

____ Older Women's League (202) 783-6686

____ National Academy of Elder Law Attorneys (529) 881-4005

____ National Association for Home Care (202) 547-7424

____ National Institute on Adult Day Care (202) 479-1200

____ National Association of Professional Geriatric Care Managers (602) 881-8008

____ Children of Aging Parents (800) 227-7294

____ Eldercare America (301) 593-1621

____ Eldercare Locator (800) 677-1116

____ Well Spouse Foundation (800) 838-0879

____ Family Services America (800) 221-2681

____ American Association of Retired Persons (800) 424-3410

____ Legal Services for the Elderly (212) 391-0120

____ National Association of Area Agencies on Aging (202) 296-8130

____ Social Security Administration (800) 772-1213

____ United Seniors Health Council (800) 637-2604

____ American Occupational Therapy Association (800) SAY-AOTA

Section 2

Mental Well-Being and Aging

Chapter 11

How Thinking Skills Change with Age

Over time, a person's thinking skills change. Some of the most common changes that come with aging include decreased IQ, reduced problem-solving ability, decreased memory, diminished attention span, and a decline in language skills. Changes in IQ are frequently seen after age 60, with significant changes noted by age 70. What doesn't seem to change is a person's ability to remember facts that don't change over time; this is called crystallized intelligence.

What to Look For
- **Thinking Speed**

  As brain cells begin to die, the brain's ability to think quickly is hampered. What used to be an efficient process now takes a lot longer. This general slowing of the central nervous system may be evident as your older loved one takes more time to think about and respond to questions.
- **Memory Skills**

  Changes can be noted in an older person's ability to recall information or details. Look for small changes in memory, like confused facts or missed details of a conversation.

- **Concentration / Attention Skills**
  Attention skills are necessary to hold a thought in mind, and also to change thoughts quickly and smoothly. "Sustained attention" is used to remember why you walked into a room, or to complete the writing of a letter. "Alternating attention" is used to shift focus quickly, such as when following the rapid shifts in a television news program. Look for an inability to hold thoughts, or difficulty shifting thoughts quickly.
- **Problem-Solving**
  After age 60, people often experience impaired problem-solving skills. Look for signs that an older person may be selecting inappropriate strategies to deal with problems. Problem-solving skills are very important when it comes to remaining safe.

Some Suggestions Include:

1. Give an older person plenty of time to process instructions or directions you have given.
2. Give instructions and directions in an appropriate setting. Older persons better understand discussions when they take place in the right environment. For example, discuss a grocery list while in the kitchen.
3. Use it or iose it. Encourage your older loved one to keep memory skills sharpened through remembering. Reminiscence is a wonderful way to practice using memory skills.
4. Be patient. Don't add stress to a situation by demanding quick responses from an older person.
5. Use helpful tools like shopping lists to assist with thinking skills.

Thinking Skills Checklist

Speak to a health care provider regarding your loved one if changes are noted in any of the following areas:

____ Tendency to get disoriented or lost in a store.

____ Inability to recall recent events.

____ Giving up meaningful hobbies.

____ Wandering or restlessness.

____ Increased agitation.

____ Missed appointments.

____ Increased isolation.

____ Confusion regarding daily routine.

____ Occasional incontinence.

____ Increased focus on the past.

____ Inability to manage personal finances.

____ Increased emotional eruptions.

____ Decreased focus on others; increased focus on self.

____ Occasional dressing difficulties such as mismatched buttons.

____ Inability to remember short lists of items.

____ Sexual inappropriateness or misconduct.

____ Confusion about surroundings.

Chapter *12*

Maintaining Thinking Skills

In middle age, when a person struggles for the right word, or hesitates in remembering a name, people laugh and say, "Well, you're having a senior moment." For seniors, however, the idea of aging without full use of one's thinking skills is frightening. Changes in thinking skills actually begin in the 20s and continue gradually throughout life. Thankfully, however, wisdom and life experience offset most of the changes that come with aging. Seniors fear that forgetfulness leads to dementia. It does not.

Dementia is a progressive disorder that leads to impaired thinking, impaired learning skills, and changes in memory, mood, personality, and judgment. It is most commonly seen in people over age 65, but is not a normal part of aging; in fact, only a small percentage of people over age 65 are diagnosed with dementia. Less than 8% of the total population aged 65 and older suffer from dementia. The incidence of dementia increases with age; up to 20% of people aged 80 and older may have dementia (Select Committee on Aging statistics). Again, older persons do not normally suffer from dementia.

Common age-related changes in thinking skills include:

- Decrease in the speed with which information is stored and retrieved.
- Change in long-term and short-term memory.
- Increased difficulty with language tasks such as finding the right word.
- Increased difficulty concentrating on tasks when outside distractions are present.
- Changes in sensory awareness and perceptual skills, needed to respond quickly to the environment.

Many research studies are exploring what factors affect thinking skills in aging persons. This chapter looks at some of the research findings in an effort to identify what families can do to help maintain thinking skills in older loved ones.

Research Findings on Thinking Skills in Aging
Many of the changes in thinking skills in older life can be handled by dealing with **non-genetic factors** like lifestyle and psychosocial or mental fitness. A person living in a stimulating environment may have more of an opportunity to exercise his or her mental abilities. Training and practice can improve some types of cognitive functioning. Persons who have enjoyed mental challenges throughout their life, like hobbies, travel, reading, stimulating work, and continued learning, seem to better maintain levels of cognitive functioning. It sometimes takes older persons longer to learn, but they retain information as well as younger persons.

The MacArthur Study of Successful Aging found that **education** was the best predictor of cognitive function. The more education a person had, the less he or she experienced a decline in thinking skills. The second most important predictor involved **lung function**. Lung function, along with exercise, enhances memory. **Strenuous physical activity** was the third predictor of cognitive functioning, followed by **self-efficacy**, which is a person's feeling about their ability to influence what happens to them in daily life.

Physical fitness affects the ability to shift from one mental task to another. Formerly sedentary adults aged 60 to 75, who began a regular aerobic walking program, improved their attention skills.

A **diet** high in antioxidants may reduce the risk of developing Alzheimer's disease by as much as 25%. Many fresh fruits and vegetables contain antioxidants such as beta-carotene, vitamin A, vitamin C, and vitamin E. The energy restriction theory suggests that caloric restriction prolongs life after age 40.

A person's **social support** affects their mental performance in older age. Persons who never marry are at twice the risk of developing dementia. Older persons living in communities have lower rates of diagnosable depression than younger adults .

Research using animals suggests that a stimulating environment may affect brain development. The role of early education as it relates to long-term cognitive functioning is being studied.

Suggestions for Maintaining Thinking Skills in Aging Loved Ones

- **Maintain healthy lifestyle routines** to counter the risk of diabetes and high blood pressure.
- **Establish ways to reduce stress.** Feeling overwhelmed affects the ability to recall information.
- **Get enough sleep.** Sleep disturbances impair the brain's ability to function. Address environmental factors like noise or an uncomfortable mattress to help improve sleep. Limit the intake of caffeine in daily diet.
- **Get support.** Feelings of loss, grief, and overwhelming sadness interfere with thinking skills. Mental health professionals and support groups addressing the needs of seniors may be helpful.
- **Consult a physician** if a sudden onset of confusion occurs. Many physical factors, including medication

interaction and depression, can contribute to impaired thinking skills.

- **Use daily tools** such as a "To Do" list or calendar to help organize time responsibilities. Creating a simple, practical system frees the brain from having to manage an overload of information.
- **Exercise daily** to improve circulation and increase blood flow to the brain. Consult a physician before beginning an exercise program.

Chapter *13*

Understanding Dementia and Alzheimer's

Y ou're noticing missed details, memory lapses, and increased confusion in your loved one...is this a normal part of aging? Is this Alzheimer's? Is something else going on that is contributing to this change?

Aging brings numerous changes in the body and mind. Normal aging includes:

- Impaired memory skills.
- Decreased speed in processing information.
- Reduced problem-solving ability.
- Impaired concentration and attention skills.

Dementia is a condition that affects a person's thinking skills, memory, personality, and behavior. It is most commonly seen in people over age 65, but is not a normal part of aging; in fact, only a small percentage of people over age 65 are diagnosed with dementia. Less than 8% of the total population aged 65 and older have dementia. The incidence of dementia increases with age; up to 20% of people aged 80 and older may have dementia (Select Committee on Aging statistics). Only a small percentage of seniors acquire dementia.

Dr Barry Reisburg developed an Alzheimer's Assessment called the Functional Assessment Staging for Alzheimer's (FAST), which breaks down the condition into seven stages as follows:

Stage One
No functional problems are observed yet. An adverse reaction to eye drops may be the only symptom.

Stage Two
Symptoms: work difficulty; some forgetfulness noted.
Functional Ability: can still plan a dinner party.

Stage Three
Symptoms: avoids new challenges; gets lost; forgets series of steps; decreased ability to recall names of new acquaintances.
Functional Ability: difficulty traveling to new locations; can't handle demanding work.

Stage Four (Mild Dementia)
Symptoms: decreased ability to perform complex tasks such as managing finances, but remains oriented to knowing time and place.
Functional Ability: requires daily supervision; should wear an identification bracelet; may be easily exploited so needs protection for safety; should use lists for shopping.

Stage Five (Moderate Dementia)
Symptoms: can't survive independently; disoriented to time and place; able to feed and toilet independently.
Functional Ability: should not drive a car; requires assistance in choosing appropriate attire; may let spoiled food collect without noticing.

Stage Six (Moderately Severe Dementia)
Symptoms: bowel and bladder incontinence, interrupted sleep cycle, forgets names of even close friends and family members.

<u>Functional Ability:</u> requires constant supervision and structure; assistance needed for toileting, bathing, and eating.

Stage Seven (Severe Dementia)
<u>Symptoms:</u> speech is limited to one-word responses; decreased ability to walk; difficulty holding head up; difficulty sitting up; inability to smile.
<u>Functional Ability:</u> requires 24-hour care.

The most common form of dementia is the Alzheimer's type. Symptoms of dementia such as confusion, disorientation, memory impairment and agitation can occur along with physical or mental health conditions including:

- Stroke
- Drug abuse or toxicity
- Brain tumor
- Traumatic brain injury
- Thyroid problems
- Nutritional deficiency of folic acid
- Alcoholism
- Infectious disease such as meningitis, syphilis, and AIDS

The onset of dementia can occur rapidly or slowly. Depending on the cause, dementia may be treated and the symptoms reversed. An accurate diagnosis to explain mental changes is critical. The evaluation process should include:

- Information on a person's family background, including family members who may have experienced dementia.
- Complete medical history.
- Tests to rule out undiagnosed medical conditions. Tests may include blood and urine tests, CT scans, MRI, functional tests to determine problem areas, written and oral tests to measure changes in a person's thinking

skills, and evaluation to rule out psychological conditions.

Suggestions for Common Problems in Dementia

1. Anxiety and agitation may occur because a person no longer understands what is happening. It is important to keep in mind that pain may also cause agitation. Once pain or discomfort such as hunger is ruled out, try to distract the person with dementia with an enjoyable activity.

2. Hostility, frustration and anger may result from an inability to understand what is going on. Support groups are valuable in helping to address issues of anger.

3. Wandering and pacing are frequently seen as a person with dementia feels a need to move. Safe activities may include regular supervised walks or physical movement to music.

4. Rummaging may occurs as the person is searching for familiarity in the midst of confusion. Handing them familiar objects like photos may have a calming effect.

5. Suspiciousness may be seen as the person experiences fear of the unknown. With memory loss, even family members may not be recognized and may be perceived as strangers.

6. Don't try to challenge a person experiencing delusions or hallucinations. Speak calmly and with a tone of understanding.

7. Sun Downers Syndrome is a condition that may occur each evening as nighttime draws near. Increased confusion and disorientation may be noted. Try closing the blinds or shades and illuminating the room with light.

Treatment Approaches

Reversible dementia may be dealt with through:
- Adjustments in medication. New medications on the market have been effective in enhancing thinking skills.
- Treatment for existing conditions such as alcoholism, infection, or depression.
- Dietary changes to stabilize nutrition.
- Support groups to enhance social stimulation and functioning.

Irreversible dementia may be dealt with through:
- Medications to address anxiety, agitation, disturbed sleep, and impaired thinking skills.
- Therapy intervention, such as occupational therapy, to help develop structure in daily routines. Occupational therapists are skilled at helping individuals maximize their ability to function in and outside the home.
- Support groups for individuals and their families, to better understand the changes that may occur with dementia.
- Psychiatric day treatment can help persons with dementia to better understand their illness. Specially trained clinicians address coping strategies and behavior management.
- Home health services such as visiting nurses, physical therapists, occupational therapists, home maker services, and home health aides may be helpful in assisting with home needs such as self-care, eating, bathing, dressing, and meaningful leisure activities to help cope with stress and frustration.
- Adult day programs for persons with dementia. These programs can offer much needed respite for caregivers, and at the same time, offer a safe, stimulating environment for persons with dementia

Chapter 14

Memory Strategies

Memory and learning are thinking skills that go hand-in-hand. They involve the process of experiencing, storing, and recalling information. Memory can be divided into several types by the length of time involved: short-term memory, long-term memory, and remote memory. Each type of memory plays a unique role in everyday functioning. Listed below are examples of each:

Type of Memory	Everyday Example
Short-term memory	Learning the name of a new person
Long-term memory	Remembering the date of the last doctor's appointment
Remote memory	Memories of childhood home

Memory involves not only how a person recalls information, but also how they experienced an event and then processed and stored the information. Problems can occur at any stage of this process. A senior experiencing "memory problems" may be having difficulty absorbing information when hearing loss is present. They may also be having difficulty storing information, or recalling the information once it has been stored. The research seems to indicate that aging affects all areas of the memory process (Davis and Kirkland, 1986).

Types of Memory Loss
Memory loss can occur with normal aging, with dementia, and with frontal lobe brain disorders. Normal aging affects short-term and long-term memory, but rarely affects remote memory. Dementia is reversible in five percent of patients, especially those affected by thyroid disorders; however, for the other ninety-five percent of patients, memory loss is irreparable. Dementia can be caused by head trauma, infection, alcohol damage, tumors, and disorders of the brain. Frontal lobe disorders can also be caused by trauma or injury to the head, tumors, and alcoholism. The first signs of frontal lobe disorders are personality changes, then memory impairment, along with impaired judgment, lack of inhibition, and decreased ability to plan.

Research Findings
1. The brain can regenerate its cells in the part of the brain involved in learning and creating new memories. People can grow new brain cells well into old age. Brain cells seem to maintain their health during active learning.
2. Sensory experiences like physical exercise and a stimulating learning environment can trigger brain cell growth in mice. These experiences also seem to increase the life span of existing cells.
3. Attention, not memory, affects how people recall information. People recalled information only when they were paying attention as the information was presented.
4. By improving cardiovascular fitness, functions such as planning, scheduling, and attention could also be improved in aging persons. These functions are vital to memory. These improvements required increased

cardiovascular fitness, and did not occur with toning or stretching alone.

5. Alzheimer's disease may involve deterioration in attention skills, rather than memory. Some "false memory" experiences may come as a result of difficulties in retrieving stored information.

6. Although still in the early stages, some research suggests some memory-training programs may help seniors avoid a decline in thinking skills. Research by Dr Lawrence Katz at Duke University shows that people can fight off the effects of mental aging by altering daily routines and combining emotional experiences with those that involve the five senses.

7. Can't quite remember that name? Research shows that "tip-of-the-tongue" memory moments begin as early as forty, and become more frequent with age. According to Deborah Burke, PhD, the problem is not with remembering the name, but rather with remembering the sound of a specific name. Training which associates words or a name with sounds may be promising for many.

8. Scientists believe that estrogen may play a role in preventing the decline of thinking skills in menopausal women. Estrogen seems to support the functions of the hippocampus, the part of the brain responsible for learning and memory.

9. A decline in memory and thinking skills caused by stroke may be reversed, if the patient is given blood clot-dissolving medications very soon after symptoms begin, usually within three hours. Stroke, which is caused by a blockage in or rupture of blood vessels in the brain, affects a quarter of a million people each year and is the third leading cause of death in the United States, behind cancer and heart disease. Symptoms include language difficulty, weakness, numbness, severe headache, and problems with vision. Risk factors that contribute to stroke include high blood pressure, smoking, alcoholism, and diabetes.

10. People with moderate Alzheimer's disease who were given high doses of vitamin E experienced a slowing of the progression of Alzheimer's by seven months. Specifically, selegiline, vitamin E, or a combination of the two delayed death, loss of the ability to do daily activities, moves into nursing homes, and progression to severe dementia.

11. Vitamin E may protect against cognitive impairment in older persons.

Suggestions for Maintaining and Enhancing Memory

- Sleep deprivation can contribute to memory impairment. Ensure that older loved ones are getting adequate sleep by addressing obstacles that interfere with sleep, including pain, medications, caffeine, fear, light, and noise.
- Sudden memory impairment along with confusion can occur with a number of medical conditions, including urinary tract infection, blood sugar irregularity, and head trauma caused by a fall. Get immediate medical attention for seniors who suddenly display memory loss and confusion.
- Vitamin deficiency, such as of vitamin B12 and vitamin E, can contribute to health decline and cognitive decline. Consult a medical doctor to better determine the correct vitamin routine.
- Early and continued education throughout life seems to affect brain structure and help prevent disease. Make it a goal to continue life-long learning. Senior centers and community adult education programs offer numerous classes to help with this process.
- Enhance stimulation of the senses by altering the type of music you listen to, adding new spices to meals, switching the type of lotion / soap used, and driving with the window rolled down. All these experiences vary the routine of everyday tasks.

- When information is presented to a senior, make certain that eye contact is made and that distractions in the room are eliminated. This will enhance learning and recall.
- Regular cardiovascular exercise for seniors, such as swimming and walking, improves the amount of oxygen and blood flow to the brain. Help seniors work with their doctor to establish a regular cardiovascular fitness program.
- Memory training programs are becoming more and more available. While the research is not conclusive as to what type of memory training is most effective, the research is conclusive that learning can and should continue well into old age. The "use it or lose it" mentality seems accurate.
- Encourage seniors to talk about something else when they are not able to recall a specific name or fact. It seems that by shifting attention to something else, the correct name, fact, or word will come automatically.
- Discuss vitamin therapy with your family physician to determine the correct dosage and use of vitamins, including antioxidants, which have been effective in countering the effects of aging.
- Memory difficulties can contribute to poor nutrition, impaired ability to keep safe, decreased independence in daily routines, and improper medication consumption. Consult an occupational therapist to evaluate and treat loved ones with impaired memory.
- Many creative reminder systems are available on the market today. One is the use of a pager that alerts seniors when it is time to take medication, keep appointments, eat regular meals, and tune into regular television shows. The system is simple and personalized, giving seniors back their independence.
- Stress contributes to memory loss by releasing a chemical called cortisol that is harmful to brain cells. Addressing stress with relaxation techniques, prayer

and meditation, and exercise helps to maintain mental capabilities.

- Memory loss may be accompanied by a decreased ability to plan. Routines for meals, activities, and medication are vital in maintaining function. Day programs can assist seniors living in the community with regular meals, activities, and medication administration.
- Activities such as travel, gardening, and knitting have been shown to contribute to successful aging.
- Head trauma can account for memory loss. Fall prevention is critical in protecting against head injuries.
- The Food and Drug Administration have approved several medications which can help maintain memory skills. These medications, however, have not been shown to reverse damage.
- The risk of stroke can be lessened by proper diet, exercise, and the reduction of stress in daily life.
- Forgetfulness is not a sign of dementia. The rule of thumb is that if a person recognizes that they can't remember a name, they do not have dementia; rather, they are simply experiencing difficulty recalling. Recall can be affected by grief, depression, fatigue, and stress. A person with dementia is not aware of recall difficulties, because memories are erased forever from the brain's functions.

Memory Checklist

Families should look for the following signs of impaired memory:

____ Missed meals leading to weight loss.
____ Skipped dosages of medication.
____ Inappropriate choice of clothing in inclement weather.
____ Missed doctor's appointments or important dates.
____ Confusion as to the day of the week and the date.
____ Repeated conversations.
____ Appliances left on or refrigerator door left open.
____ Decreased awareness of soiled clothing.
____ Increased need for supervision and structure.
____ Decreased ability to plan for shopping trips.
____ Missed calculations in checkbook.
____ Small errors in daily routines.
____ Skipped family traditions.
____ Decreased ability to focus attention.
____ Decreased ability to recall names and phone numbers.
____ Need for more structured routine.

Chapter 15

Aging and Addiction Concerns

Addictions among older persons often go undetected. Estimates of the number of persons over age 65 with dependency problems range from half a million to over two million in the United States. Persons over age 65 take, on average, more than three prescription drugs and more than seven non-prescription drugs on a regular basis. While this group makes up less than twenty percent of the US population, they use between 25 and 33% of the prescription medications consumed each year. Alcohol-related problems affect 20 to 50% of nursing home residents. One study indicated that 14% of seniors arriving at the emergency room abuse alcohol. Alcohol problems can be compounded by over-the-counter and prescription drug use. Recent data indicates that more hospitalizations can be attributed to alcohol-related disorders than to heart attacks.

Factors that Contribute to Misuse and Abuse of Drugs
Older persons may experience significant loss in their later years. This may include loss of self-esteem, loss of energy, loss of loved ones and life partners, loss of memory, loss of financial security, loss of hope, and loss of full independence. These losses contribute to the risk of alcohol and other drug abuse.

Medication misuse in older persons occurs for many reasons. Many older people associate medications with feeling better. This can lead to the erroneous thinking that if one pill makes them feel good, a second or third will make them feel great. Medications tend to stay longer in the body of an older person. Medications may interact with each another when not taken properly. Persons who hesitate in asking questions of their doctor or pharmacist may not understand the medication instructions. Vision problems often interfere with reading package labels and can lead to misuse of medications.

Alcohol abuse may have been a problem earlier in the life of an aging person, or may begin in later years in an effort to cope with pain and loss. Many people believe that alcohol use contributes to many falls and accidents. Alcohol affects the body of an older person differently than that of a younger person, due to changes in metabolism and body water volume as people age. Families are often hesitant to confront their older loved ones because they want to avoid embarrassing them. This is unfortunate because treatment can be very successful and is available in most communities.

Signs of Alcohol Abuse in Older Persons

Because older persons drive less often, they are less likely to be stopped for driving under the influence. Likewise, because many are retired, job-related problems do not occur. Accidents, falls, bone fractures, confusion, personality changes, and malnutrition are indicators of drug and alcohol abuse. Changes in the body's functioning due to abuse can include liver damage, impaired thinking skills, high blood pressure, and weakness.

Prevention and Treatment Suggestions for Families

1. Encourage seniors to not be shy about asking for help and information about the proper use of medications. Seniors should be well educated about the purpose of each prescription.

2. Fill all prescriptions at one pharmacy so medications and dosages can be easily tracked.
3. One physician should coordinate the prescriptions of other team specialists to reduce the risk of drug interactions.
4. Ask the doctor to write clear instructions for taking medications. Persons with memory or hearing difficulties may miss important details if they are not written out.
5. Use a calendar for proper medication dosing.
6. Encourage older loved ones to find meaningful activities to bolster self-esteem and help them cope with grief and loss in a healthy way.
7. Group treatment provides peer support to address not only the addiction problems, but also the feelings that contribute to the abuse of drugs and alcohol.

Treatment Approaches

Treatment can take place on three levels: inpatient treatment, outpatient treatment, and self-help support groups. Many people initially need the support of inpatient treatment as they withdraw from the overuse of alcohol or drugs. This process is called detoxification. Rehabilitation on an outpatient basis generally follows detoxification. Outpatient treatment can take place either in groups specially designed to address the needs of seniors, or on an individual basis with mental health professionals trained in addiction. Self-help groups include organizations like Alcoholics Anonymous or Narcotics Anonymous.

Addiction Checklist

Start by contacting a family physician if you are concerned about possible abuse or misuse of drugs and alcohol by your older loved one. Many conditions can produce similar symptoms, so the involvement of a physician is necessary to properly diagnose a problem.

Signs include:

___   Falls and accidents.

___   Weakness.

___   Unsteadiness.

___   Confusion.

___   Weight loss.

___   Broken bones.

___   Depression.

___   Personality change.

___   Social withdrawal.

___   Isolation.

___   Secrecy or guardedness.

Chapter 16

Organizational Skills for Seniors

Organizational skills have many facets; among these is an awareness of time, attention span, and self-management skills. Organizational skills are critical for medication management, meal preparation, financial management, healthy daily routines of sleep/rest and productivity, and independent functioning in the community.

The *Thinking Skills Workbook* by Carter, Caruso, and Languirand defines the need for these skills in daily life to "help auditory concentration, scheduling, awareness and the general organization of one's life (p. 4)." During younger years, active, busy people are aware of getting things done and the passage of time during activities. Gradual changes may occur during the natural aging process that affects this awareness.

Carter *et al* suggest that illness or hospitalization affect the engagement in familiar, daily routines. The new, unfamiliar routines may bring feelings of disorientation, frustration, and withdrawal. Apathy and confusion may arise, as people no longer pay attention to the environmental cues of time. Anyone who has spent significant time at a hospital bedside is aware of these changes. My family referred to the many hours that seemed to pass unnoticed, when we were away from familiar tasks, routines, and responsibility, as "hospital time."

Paying bills on time and making regular bank deposits are often indicators of how independently an older person is functioning. Difficulty in these areas does not necessarily mean that a person cannot live alone safely, but it does indicate that some level of support is needed. Many communities have volunteer services that provide assistance to seniors with check writing and bill paying. Managing important information, such as the dates and times of appointments, can be difficult for persons of any age, and especially difficult for older persons with organizational challenges.

Routines

While daily routines provide a predictable, structured approach to daily tasks, routines vary from person to person. Some people bathe every morning, some every evening, some once a week, some shower every two days, some sponge bathe from a sink, etc. Not only do routines provide familiarity to each day or part of a day, they also help seniors remember to do specific tasks, such as take medication, get rest, etc. at appropriate times.

Injury or impairment in aging can bring an upset to long-established routines. New routines are not easily established and can be exhausting. The key to any daily routine for an older person is their motivation to occupy themselves in meaningful ways. In order for older people to stay healthy and energetic, meals and medications need to be taken regularly. No matter how hard a family member might try, if an older loved one does not perceive a task or activity as meaningful or necessary, it may not get done. Understanding, from this perspective, the decisions your loved one makes is important.

Suggestions for Daily Routines:

1. Understand what is important to your loved one by asking pertinent questions before trying to develop routines with them. If staying healthy is important to them, they may be willing to discuss medication routines or exercise routines. If independence is more important, they may be willing to look at how home

safety can help prevent falls, and may facilitate their remaining independent in their own home longer. Put yourself in their shoes and see that different people value different things. Routines are only successful if they reflect what is important to us.

2. Have the older person wear a large-faced watch that is easily seen and read. This gives a person an awareness of his or her responsibility to manage time. Apathy can occur when a person loses awareness of time.

3. Group similar items together for daily routine tasks. For instance, daily grooming items should be in the same section of the bathroom. Medications should be grouped together. Clothing should be grouped with related items; for example, socks with shoes, raincoat with an umbrella, etc.

4. Checklists can be used to organize daily routines. A "Morning Routine" checklist can be developed to help prompt a senior to accomplish daily self-care responsibilities, while minimizing frustration.

5. Consider having your older loved one pay bills through automatic deduction services at the local bank to simplify or eliminate monthly check writing.

Scheduling

In a fast-paced world, life balance is challenging for all. It is especially difficult for an older person who is not thinking or moving quite as quickly as he or she did as a younger person. Healthy schedules involve a balance of work and play, responsibility and relaxation, socialization and solitude. Healthy schedules should include these basic areas:

Personal Care	Work /Productivity
Grooming / hygiene Spiritual expression Exercise Nutritious meals Medication routines Sleep	Volunteer work Home management Housework Chores Shopping Finances
Leisure / Relaxation	**Socialization**
Hobbies Crafts Sports Entertainment Creativity Journaling	Friends Family Clubs Organizations Worship Helping others Companionship

Schedules change as priorities change, but are helpful to an older person in achieving life balance. Every person, young or old, can set and achieve goals; a schedule offers small, achievable steps to meet important life balance goals. For instance, seeing and being with other people is important. A goal might be to get out of the house twice a week. A set schedule reflecting these goals might include worship one day per week, and a senior center activity on a second day. Establishing a weekly schedule eliminates the decision-making that often keeps a senior at home. Establishing transportation for these activities also acts as an encouragement. Daily contact with others helps relieve the fear that no one will notice if something traumatic happens. Regular schedules for communication like phone calls are an easy way to encourage continued, meaningful activity.

Suggestions For Scheduling
1. Review calendar entries the night before to better plan for the next day.

2. Help seniors understand when they have the most energy. Schedule the most demanding activities during these hours.
3. Schedule time for rest and relaxation each day.
4. Divide large tasks like cleaning into smaller segments, to be done over a longer period of time.
5. Schedule time for play and entertainment each day.
6. Help seniors use less time and energy each day by delegating unwanted chores such as yard work, etc.
7. Maintain regular sleep patterns each night.
8. Improve sleep by scheduling enough physical activity and stimulation during the day.
9. Leave plenty of room in daily schedules for when things don't go as planned.
10. Plan to arrive 15 minutes early for appointments, so you can arrive refreshed and relaxed.

Calendars

The need for reminders or cues varies from person to person, and changes as thinking skills decline. Most of us need an alarm going off to wake in the morning. Some people are naturally structured with their time and activities, while others are more spontaneous. The use of a calendar is effective for both types of people. Calendars help to organize routines. They relieve stress, as a person no longer has to remember detailed schedules for each day, week, and month. They enhance enjoyment of meaningful activities as anticipated events draw near. They alleviate confusion and stress reactions caused by missed appointments.

Suggestions Regarding the Use of Calendars

1. Purchase large, write-on / wipe-off calendars for seniors to use.
2. Use different color pens to distinguish different entries such as holidays, appointments, and recreational activities.
3. Encourage seniors to review the calendar events for the next day before going to bed at night.

4. Use calendars to set goals, such as getting out of the house more often or maintaining a fitness routine, and to monitor progress on these goals.

5. Help older loved ones evaluate which activities stimulate them the most, which are the most relaxing, which are the most anticipated, which are the most dreaded, and which improve how they feel about themselves.

6. Medication calendars can be used daily to ensure proper medication dosing. When medication errors increase in frequency, alternative medication reminder systems should be explored through the local visiting nurse association or senior service center.

Organizational Skills Checklist

Use this list to help evaluate your older loved one's ability to organize their life.

____ In case of emergency, my older loved one is able to quickly contact family, police, neighbors, friends, and his/her doctor using an emergency phone list in his/her wallet and posted by every telephone at home.

____ He/she carries a current list of medications, along with the pharmacy name, the physician's name, and the required dosages.

____ He/she wears an emergency medical bracelet or tag to identify health information important in case of emergency.

____ He/she can recite his/her address, phone number, and name independently, and carries identification in case of emergency.

____ He/she pays bills on time with no account overdrafts.

____ Checks are written without error.

____ Medications are taken according to the prescription. He/she understands proper dosing and rarely skips or confuses medication.

____ Medications are organized and clearly labeled. Reminder or travel medication boxes are easy for seniors to open and use without confusion.

____ He/she has delegated household tasks that are no longer satisfying or are too demanding, such as housework or yard work.

Section 3

Emotional Well-Being and Aging

Chapter 17

The Fears of Growing Older

Aging causes fears to surface for the individual as well as the family. Successful aging involves many facets including the ability to talk honestly about fear and the ability to identify ways to overcome fear. The fact remains that people are living longer, healthier, more independent lives than they did even twenty years ago. In 1982, 6.2% of the nation's elderly lived in nursing homes, while by 1999 the number had dropped to 3.4%. Between 1990 and 2000, the U.S. Census Bureau reports a 38% increase in the number of seniors over age 85, with a decrease in the number of chronically disabled older Americans. New challenges and underlying fears surface as our society ages. Discussed below are some of the current fears being felt by seniors.

Falling
F-A-L-L is a four-letter word for seniors; falling is a looming fear for older persons, especially those who have experienced a fall previously. The fear of falling is so strong that it may keep a person from going out of doors, getting out of bed, or exploring new places. When families observe a change in behavior or attitude about going out, moving around normally, or completing daily routines, fear of falling may be present. The services of an occupational therapist are helpful to "fall-

proof" a home. Seniors can learn new, safe ways to accomplish daily chores and routines and minimize the risk of falls. Home adaptation is a growing industry that allows seniors to stay at home longer.

Being Alone

Loneliness is scary and can occur with or without an accompanying feeling of sadness. Recognizing the core concern is key to resolving the fear. Seniors may fear that something bad will happen if they are by themselves. Will they be forgotten? Will they be ignored? Will anyone notice if they have fallen? Families sometimes describe their loved one as being more demanding or draining when this fear is present. Family members who have difficulty watching their older loved ones age may stay away out of discomfort. Working out a schedule of contact or visits that are agreeable and achievable for all can help minimize this fear. Mark calls and visits on a calendar so that your loved one can recall past visits and anticipate upcoming ones. The use of a calendar can avoid the "You never call or visit me" response that families often hear.

Becoming a Burden to Others

In aging, this becomes a double-edged sword, as seniors are afraid both of being a burden to others, and of being ignored. Sometimes careful planning can alleviate this fear. Facilities that provide varying levels of care for older persons are ideal. Seniors may initially desire independent apartment living, then gradually decide to free themselves of meal preparation by stepping up to a semi-independent level of care, which provides a hot meal at noontime. Assisted Living provides a variety of services, ranging from meal preparation to cleaning, and recreation to medication reminders. Choosing the right facility with an eye to the future can reduce the fear that a senior will end up burdening others with their care needs.

Running Out of Money

Seniors may hesitate to talk openly about financial fears, but direct communication about the present, and financial goals for the future is imperative. Families can assist seniors in several ways. Firstly, automating direct deposits and recurring bills can help seniors avoid missed payments. Secondly, important financial and legal documents can be organized in one location where they can be easily accessed should an emergency occur. Thirdly, assist older loved ones in taking advantage of senior discounts for medications, groceries, and senior housing. A hint to families: just because a person has physical limitations does not mean he or she cannot make his or her own financial decisions. Families should consider assisting their loved one in making financial decisions, rather than taking over financial responsibility.

Becoming Sick

Seniors may equate a person's worth with their ability to remain productive. During the war years, our country had little sympathy for those who couldn't "pull their weight." Unfortunately, this is a very limiting belief for aging persons. Aging frequently brings with it a decline in both physical and cognitive abilities. Families can work to encourage older persons to focus not on their disabilities, but rather on their abilities. Seniors can live highly purposeful lives. Older persons possess a wealth of knowledge and life experience; many communities are recognizing this fact and implementing intergenerational programs that pair older persons with young people. Volunteer programs like the Senior Corps of Retired Executives (SCORE) tap into this diverse knowledge base and put it to good use in our society. Families should help seniors identify how they can feel productive and connected to the world around them.

Losing Independence

"If I can't do for myself, then life ain't worth living," was the sentiment of one senior who was assessing a recent decline in her ability to function safely at home. Everyone seems to want to be able to take care of him or herself. The early words of a two-year-old are, "I do it!" This feeling is echoed throughout our lifespan. Unfortunately, many seniors equate needing some help with failure; families sometimes contribute to this fear by refusing to get assistance when early signs of needing more help are evident. Families sometimes ignore the early signs, then rush in and take over, creating feelings of resentment and anger in their older loved ones. Problems can best be solved with seniors and families working together to find solutions.

Losing Control

One of the biggest fears that seniors express is their fear of losing control of their own life. Changes in the body and mind do come naturally with aging, and these changes can seem overwhelming for older persons. Something like losing bladder control can cause major changes in a person's daily routine. They no longer feel that venturing out to visit friends is worth the risk of embarrassment. Dignity comes from being able to make independent decisions, and families need to allow older loved ones the right to make as many decisions as possible with dignity and independence. Conflict often comes into play over issues like driving safety, when the desired independence of a senior is in opposition to what others deem best for the older person. Working with a coach or social worker can help families and seniors work through these issues.

Feeling Unsafe Outside the Home

Seniors may become increasingly housebound as their fear of injury or attack rises. Reading the newspaper or listening to disturbing news reports of violence exacerbates their feelings of helplessness. As a result of this fear, seniors may decide they can keep themselves safe at home and may no longer want to venture out as much. Helping seniors take advantage of door-to-door transportation services and senior programs through the community senior center will help alleviate these fears.

Unfinished Plans and Dreams
Older persons should continue to set quarterly goals that can be broken down into monthly and weekly goals. Goals should address many areas of life including spiritual expression, physical health, social stimulation, financial health, and emotional well-being. By setting clear, attainable goals, seniors can alleviate the fear of dying with unfulfilled dreams. Families can assist seniors by asking what could be done to improve their quality of life. Many seniors find that if they create a rewarding experience every day, the future takes care of itself.

C h a p t e r **18**

Transition and Change for the Older Person

R etirement is often thought of as the golden years, but for many seniors, the golden years feel tarnished. Instead of more freedom, more leisure time, and fewer financial constraints, these years are frequently filled with unrealized goals, disappointment, and constant change and adjustment. Many older persons and their loved ones are blindsided when these changes occur. Change brings an adjustment in routine, an uncertainty about the future, fear of the unknown and the unpredictable, and a recognition of lack of control. Facing the challenges empowered by skills, strength, and life experience will make adjustment easier for your senior loved one. Out of challenge can come new ways of coping with and adapting to life for both older persons and their families.

Transition and Aging
For seniors, the transition from working years to retirement can cause a drop in self-esteem. No longer feeling as productive, seniors may be at a loss for what a meaningful daily routine should look like. In addition, loss of energy or health can increase the challenge. Becoming more dependent on others and not wanting to ask for help may cause resentment. For families busy managing their own responsibilities, seeing their older loved ones decline in

physical or mental well-being may cause feelings of guilt or anxiety. Families walk a tightrope between wanting to help, and not wanting to step on others' toes. Adult children often feel vulnerable themselves as they see their older loved ones become more dependent. Knowing when and how to help is the topic of discussion in this chapter.

Change and transition are difficult for many. It is said that the only things that like change are vending machines and babies! Routines become comfortable and familiar, providing a level of safety. Holding on to the comfortable routines that each day brings empowers an older person to feel in control. Change and transition often undermine a sense of control, which is critical for self-esteem.

Goals for successful aging should involve rewarding daily routines, healthful environments, and meaningful relationships. These goals do not change as aging takes place. Instead, adjustments are made in how they are achieved. Families and seniors should work together to establish basic goals for a rewarding, purposeful senior life. An older person should be involved in every decision that affects his or her life, unless he or she no longer has the mental ability to do so. Two big areas of decision-making involve where to live and what to do with each day.

Where to Live
Most older persons want to remain as independent as possible. Many desire to live in their family home. Living alone at home is fine until safety or health issues become a concern. Options to consider at that time include home services to help with cleaning, shopping, and gardening, and home health services which can assist with showering or bathing, meal preparation, and medication management. A person's home provides more than just shelter; it should be a place of comfort, safety, and well-being. A home safety evaluation should be completed by an occupational therapist to help prevent falls. Adaptations can be made to make daily tasks and chores easier and safer.

Frequently, loneliness is a major problem for older persons. Living alone may not provide enough social stimulation and interaction. With decreased energy and lack of transportation, seniors can become isolated and depressed. Living alone may no longer be a healthful environment for them. Options include community senior housing, taking on a housemate or roommate, or various levels of assisted living. Each of these options has advantages and disadvantages to consider. Working together, seniors and their families should discuss all possible options. Transition and adjustment is easier if feelings are discussed, community resources are considered, and seniors feel they have input in decisions that affect them.

Meaningful Daily Routines

The senior years can provide more free time than earlier seasons of life, when family and career responsibilities filled each day. This extra time has advantages and disadvantages. The advantages include more time to pursue leisure interests and more time to accomplish daily tasks, which can take longer in the senior years. The disadvantages are that older persons may set fewer goals and have less energy to spend purposefully. Empty time can lead to disillusionment and loneliness.

Seniors today are pioneers in many ways. They are living longer, are better-educated, healthier, and more culturally aware than earlier generations. In 1950, 46% of men remained in the work force past the age of 65, whereas today less than 16% continue to work beyond age 65. As life expectancy increases, the need to create meaningful routines throughout later life will challenge every senior. Research indicates that several factors contribute to successful aging, including mental stimulation, close social connections, intimacy with others, maintaining a sense of purpose in life, regular spiritual expression, physical exercise, and challenging activities such as traveling, knitting, and gardening.

Many community resources offer programs geared to assist with successful aging. Community senior centers provide a varied program of peer interaction, continued learning, and recreational stimulation. Libraries and community park and recreation programs offer a regular schedule of diverse activities, from line dancing to computer skills. Centers of worship may provide hot meals and transportation to senior programs. Getting out of one's normal environment helps to relieve boredom and gives seniors something to look forward to. Even older persons living in assisted care facilities benefit from a change in environment and time away with family. Volunteer opportunities abound for seniors. Not only does volunteering contribute to feelings of self-esteem, but remaining connected to the needs of the community helps seniors, with their wealth of life experience and wisdom, give back to society.

Families may need to involve themselves in dealing with transportation issues. Seniors who are housebound suffer from poorer health and increased feelings of isolation. Families may also need to accompany their older loved ones when they are trying new activities or senior programs for the first time. Seniors need to be able to try a variety of activities until they find the right fit for them.

As a person's physical and mental abilities change, so will the type of activities they enjoy. Day clubs and adult daycare centers offer a safe, structured environment for persons who can no longer negotiate their day independently. These programs can provide needed relief for caregivers as well.

Suggestions for Families:

1. Involve older persons in decision-making. Talk about possible options to solve problems. Visit facilities and senior centers together.
2. Research the community agencies on aging to get a sense of what services would be helpful to your loved one. Some services are publicly funded while others require private pay.
3. Consult a financial planner who specializes in aging issues to better understand how to plan for the cost of future care.
4. Local churches and places of worship offer a wide range of programs and assistance, in addition to providing for the spiritual needs of seniors.

5. Keep communication open with your older loved one. Listen carefully to the feelings behind the words.

6. Consider a senior support group or treatment program to help ease adjustment to new situations, like losing a driver's license or relocating.

7. Consult a medical doctor if families notice increased isolation, feelings of hopelessness, decreased concentration, or change in weight.

8. Assist seniors with identifying what they enjoy doing and what community activities would be of interest to them.

9. Help senior loved ones establish an achievable and rewarding weekly schedule.

10. Watch for changes in vision or hearing that might be easily remedied.

11. Watch for changes in loved ones that indicate they may need additional support with daily tasks. Look for soiled clothes, diminished personal grooming and hygiene, late bill paying or overdrafts, and an increasingly disorganized environment.

12. Talk with older family members about plans and goals for the future. Be specific and clear.

Chapter 19

Grief or Depression: Understanding the Difference

Depression is a common illness that affects not only the mind, but the body as well. While depression can affect persons of all ages, it is often more difficult to recognize in older persons. Because grief and sadness are often a normal part of the aging experience, depression can go unnoticed. If untreated, depression can lead to serious problems, including suicide.

Symptoms of depression include:

- Depressed or sad mood.
- Decreased interest or pleasure in activities.
- Change in appetite or weight.
- Sleep irregularities.
- Fatigue or loss of energy.
- Feelings of worthlessness.
- Poor concentration.
- Recurring thoughts of death or suicide.

Causes of Depression

The cause of depression is not clear, but it appears to be affected by changes in the brain's chemistry. Depression can frequently be generated by life events such as the death of a loved one, a change in physical condition, an adverse reaction to medication, an underlying medical condition, alcohol use, changes in season, financial constraints, and the need for relocation.

Changes in a person's functioning can be examined in three areas:

Feelings	Behavior	Physical Complaints
Feelings of hopelessness	Pulling away from friends and family	Fatigue
Feelings of worthlessness	Concentration difficulties	Lack of energy
Lack of enjoyment in everyday activities	Irritable mood	Change in appetite, either increased or decreased
	Memory changes	
Wanting to be alone	Changes in ability to complete daily tasks	Overall aches and pains
Wanting the pain of life to be over	Decreased grooming / hygiene	Too much or too little sleep
Sad mood most of the time		

Distinguishing depression from other conditions is imperative. Depression in older persons is often either overlooked or misdiagnosed. This can happen because normal aging can involve a change in appetite and sleep patterns, reduced energy level and endurance, and some social withdrawal.

Normal Grief	Depression
• Sadness about recent losses • Sadness about financial problems • Sadness about having to move to a new residence • Sadness about medical complications • Sadness about retirement • Lasts several weeks	• Presence of five symptoms within 2 month period • Inability to "snap out of it" • Feelings are affecting daily life and routines • Considering thoughts of death and suicide • Deterioration in quality of life and ability to enjoy daily activities

Dementia	Depression
• Person conceals memory loss • Poor recent memory but good remote memory • Progressive memory loss • Confabulates answers to questions • Insidious onset of symptoms • Easily distracted	• Person exaggerates memory loss • Variable recent and remote memory loss • Memory improves and depression lifts • Avoids answering questions • Rapid onset of condition • Depressed appearance • Little noticeable response to attempts to redirect attention

Suicide in Older Adults
Aging brings a host of difficulties to almost everyone. Suicide
is always a risk for someone who is significantly depressed.
Suicide is three times as common in persons over age 65.
Men are especially at risk between the ages of 80 and 85,
while the risk of suicide in women declines after age 65.
Fully half of all suicide attempts succeed. Risk factors for
suicide include depression, hopelessness, being a single or
widowed person living alone, previous psychiatric illness or
drug addiction, previous suicide attempt or threat, diagnosis
of organic mental illness or terminal illness. Some of the
signs to watch for are:

- Giving away of personal possessions.
- Unusual behaviors regarding planning for the future.
- Talking about suicide or a passive wish to die.
- Sudden change in mood.

Contact a mental health professional immediately if any
of the above signs are noted. Unfortunately, older persons
often resist seeking help for their feelings of depression.
Seniors may believe themselves to be either "weak" or "going
crazy" and therefore feel embarrassment when seeking help.

Four Kinds of Depression
Major Depression
A major depressive episode is a marked change in behavior
from previous functioning. It is characterized by either a
depressed mood most of the time or a decrease in pleasure.
Along with these symptoms, a person with major depression
may experience an unintentional change in weight, agitation
or lethargy, loss of energy most days, depressed mood or
irritability, decreased concentration, feelings of worthlessness,
or recurrent thoughts of death.

Dysthymia
A milder form of depression, dysthymia may go undiagnosed and untreated for years. Persons with dysthymia may suffer from depressed mood, poor appetite or overeating, decreased energy level, poor concentration, low self-esteem, and feelings of hopelessness . Diagnosis is made if symptoms have lasted more than two years.

Bipolar Disorder
This is a mood disorder that involves swings from depression to mania. Mania is characterized by inflated self-esteem, racing thoughts, decreased sleep, risky behaviors, and pressured conversation. If the first occurrence of bipolar disorder is after age 65, look for possible physical factors, tumors, or medication complications. This disorder used to be called manic-depressive disorder.

Seasonal Affective Disorder
In some people, depressive episodes occur in a regular pattern during the fall and winter months, and then seem to disappear during the spring and summer months. This disorder may be associated with seasonal changes in light.

Treatment
- Many new, effective, antidepressant medications are available by doctor's prescription. See a doctor for the proper prescription.
- Therapy is recommended to help people with depression develop better ways to cope with change and manage stress. Frequently, group therapy is more effective than individual therapy because of the peer support.
- Hospitalization can usually be avoided with early detection and proper treatment.
- Occupational therapists can assist older persons with establishing meaningful routines both in the home and community. Social and recreational goals can be established to better manage feelings of loss during aging.

- The use of artificial light may be helpful for persons with Seasonal Affective Disorder.
- In cases of severe depression, electroconvulsive therapy (ECT) may be beneficial.

Suggestions include:
1. Get professional help immediately if you think your loved one may be experiencing depression.
2. Treatment is available to reverse the symptoms of depression.
3. Depression, if untreated, can lead to serious disability or suicide.
4. Many of today's antidepressants take several weeks to be effective. Get help early for your loved one.
5. Understand that antidepressants are not addictive and are closely monitored for side effects.
6. The health care professionals who treat people with depression include:
     - Psychiatrists
     - Psychologists
     - Psychiatric social workers
     - Psychiatric nurses
     - Psychiatric occupational therapists
     - Psychotherapists
     - Psychiatric recreational therapists
        (Source: National Mental Health Association)

Contact the community mental health clinic for more information.

Chapter 20

Coping with Loss

Loss is a part of life, but as people age, it can be experienced more profoundly and can increase more rapidly than during the younger years. Losses can be divided into four separate categories: physical losses, emotional losses, spiritual losses, and social losses. Grief is an emotional process that is part of coping with loss. Even though everyone experiences grief in his or her lifetime, an older person can feel quite alone with feelings of grief as a result of loss. This chapter helps to identify steps to move beyond grief and find life after loss.

Understanding Loss and Grief

Physical Loss
Physical losses include changes that an older person experiences in his or her body or environment. These include changes such as diminished hearing, vision, memory, and flexibility; reduced energy, appetite, balance, and mobility; and difficulty achieving restful sleep, bladder control, and pain-free movement. These are just a few of the many losses that your older loved one may experience. And if those weren't enough, older persons have more difficulty physically adapting to change.

Emotional Loss

Emotional losses may include a decreased sense of freedom, choice, determination, and independence. Seniors often feel that they have lost their youth and vitality, their life roles, their family traditions, and the emotional support of friends or family. The feeling that younger, worry-free days are over is often exacerbated when older people lose their driver's license, the family home, a beloved pet, or begin to have financial difficulties.

Spiritual Loss

Spiritual losses are sometimes the most difficult to identify, and may include the loss of hope, pride, confidence, joy, faith, peace, and tranquility. Older loved ones may feel that they have lost their self-esteem, their goals, their sense of adventure, their spirit, and they may no longer see a purpose in life. It is common for seniors to feel they must let go of their dreams and hopes for the future, and to lose their sense of accomplishment.

Social Loss

Social loss includes the loss of a life partner, of friends, of the ability to feel comfortable around new people, of the perceived ability to make new friends, of belonging to a meaningful group, club, neighborhood, or social circle, and of regular contact with others. Older loved ones may show a decrease in social confidence, in social skills, in the ability to read social cues from others, and in memory, affecting relationships. Seniors also report feeling that they no longer have a connection with children or grandchildren, and no longer feel they have any power or position in the community or in society.

Symptoms of Grief

Different people experience grief differently. Individual grief reactions can vary widely, not only from person to person, but also within the same person over time. For instance, anger may be experienced early on, and then again much later in the grief process. Denial may be an initial reaction, and then follow again months later.

Some of the symptoms of grief:

1. Shock and denial help by protecting an older person from feeling initially overwhelmed. A person may describe feeling "numb" or feeling as though he or she is "in a dream."
2. Panic may set in, along with feeling fearful, overwhelmed, confused, and unable to cope. A grieving person may believe something is wrong with him or herself.
3. Physical reactions may include:
   - Crying
   - Pacing
   - Wringing hands
4. Emotional reactions may include periods of:
   - Sadness
   - Loneliness
   - Isolation
   - Hopelessness
   - Self-pity
   - Sometimes referred to as "reactive depression," these emotional reactions may serve to help a person fully accept the loss, before re-engaging in regular daily routines and activities.
5. Guilt and remorse may follow as an older person sorts through regrets and "what ifs." People who know someone who has died suddenly or been in an accident frequently struggle with replaying the experience over and over in their minds, trying to sort out what might have been done differently. Resolution of guilt and remorse help a person to accept loss.
6. Anger can be directed at God, life in general, family members who make decisions for older persons, and even at a deceased person. Often anger comes with a sense of unfairness or regret. Anger can easily be misdirected at innocent people; families will need to show compassion and patience when this happens.

7. Storytelling is an important way of dealing with grief. By reminiscing and sharing anecdotes out loud, a person begins to come to terms with loss. Telling stories also serves to bring a person closer to what was lost, whether that be a person or a physical ability. Storytelling may even include laughter and humor, alternating with tears.

8. Physical symptoms are frequently experienced for up to a year and a half after the onset of grief. These can include back pain, upset stomach, sleeplessness, and increased susceptibility to common illnesses.

Coping with Grief

On many occasions after a loss, the grieving person can benefit from the support of others. Accordingly, friends need to be ready to accept the grieving person and support them through a wide range of emotions. Group support is very effective in identifying healthy ways to manage grief. Frequently, people need help to find life after loss. Family and friends can help in many ways.

Suggestions to Help Others Cope with Loss:
Develop Good Listening Skills

- Use open-ended questions that cannot be answered with a simple "yes" or "no."
- Make sure you have enough time to listen.
- Use empathy, not sympathy. Sympathy feels condescending to the person experiencing grief.
- Avoid trying to "fix" a situation.
- Avoid giving advice or suggestions, even if asked. Just say something like, "I don't know, what do you think you ought to do?"
- Don't interrupt.
- Listen 80%, talk 20%.
- Don't be afraid of silence. Avoid the natural temptation to fill empty time.

Think Before You Speak

What NOT To Say

I know just how you feel.
Death was a blessing.
Everyone goes through this.
It all happened for the best.
You're still young.
You have your whole life ahead of you.
It was God's will.
You'll feel better tomorrow.
Call me when I can help.
Something good will come out of this.
You should look on the bright side.
It's time to put it behind you now.
Be strong!

What To Say

I'm sorry.
I'm sad for you.
How are you doing with all this?
I don't know why it happened.
What can I do for you?
I'm here and I want to listen.
Please tell me what you are feeling.
This must be hard for you.
What's the hardest part for you?
You must really be hurting.
It isn't fair, is it?
Take all the time you need.
Thank you for sharing your feelings.

Find Support for Your Loved One
- Contact your local hospital or mental health center for support groups on grieving.
- Contact your local senior center for grief groups.

Encourage the Use of Stress Management / Relaxation Techniques
- Refer to Chapter 28 entitled *Relaxation Techniques for Seniors*

Anticipate Difficult Seasons Regarding Grief and Loss
- Birthdays
- Holidays
- Anniversaries
- Family get-togethers

Coping with Loss: A Three Step Approach

Looking Back

Looking back, an older person is able to identify the strengths and courage they exhibited at other difficult times in their life. Reminiscing allows an older person to see themselves in a renewed light of courage and strength. Families can assist in the reminiscing process by helping seniors review their lives.

Some suggestions include:
- Organize old photos in albums to stimulate remote memories.
- Record a cassette tape of an older loved one answering questions about him or herself, such as "What are you most proud of in your life?" or, "What was the most challenging time in your life?" or, "What are the top ten things you have learned about life and how did you learn them?"
- Record a videotape of an older loved one walking through the family home or looking at belongings, describing items along the way.

Looking Forward

Seniors sometimes feel that goal setting is no longer valuable to them. Quite the opposite is true, actually. Goals are simply intentions of what a person wants to have happen in a day, a week, a month, or a year. A weight-loss program is the perfect example. No one loses twenty pounds in a week; it is possible, however, to lose twenty pounds over ten weeks by setting small, attainable diet and exercise goals. Setting sensible, achievable, meaningful goals helps people find reason to move forward in life.

Goals can be set for any period of time: days, weeks, months, and years. Sample goals may include:

Daily	Weekly	Monthly	Yearly
Eat 3 meals each day Call 2 friends each day Take a walk each day	Shop once a week Go to church Get out of the house twice a week	Go to a support group meeting every month Go on a senior trip once a month	Travel to see family/ friends twice a year Volunteer at a local hospital

Some questions to ask oneself regarding goal setting are:
- What do I want more of in life?
- What do I want less of in life?
- What do I want to be different about my life?
- What would make me feel better?

Living for Today

Creating meaningful daily routines helps seniors cope with grief and the feelings of loss. Without a daily routine and a goal, it is too easy to say, "I don't feel like getting up today." Daily goals can be as simple as calling two friends in a day or rearranging a drawer so that it is neater. Daily goals that may help older loved ones to cope with loss include:

- Taking a daily walk.
- Writing a note of encouragement to someone.
- Getting together with others at least three times a week.
- Taking a relaxing shower or bath.
- Going to the library.
- Having a hot lunch with friends at the Senior Center.
- Helping someone else.
- Writing a note or letter of thanks to someone.
- Building a model.
- Working on a puzzle.
- Going shopping.

Grief Checklist

Listen for some of the phrases a grieving person might say:

___ I feel like I've been cheated in life.

___ It is not fair that _____ has happened.

___ What have I done to deserve this?

___ I will never feel complete again.

___ I just don't care any more.

___ The holidays are the hardest time for me.

___ It feels just like a bad dream.

___ I'm just not thinking straight these days.

___ Why don't they know how badly I must be hurting?

___ How can I go on like nothing has happened?

___ Will I ever feel better?

___ All I feel is pain. My whole body hurts more than ever.

___ I just can't stop crying.

___ I'm afraid if I go something will remind me of _____.

___ I feel empty inside.

___ I never know when it will hit me unexpectedly.

___ What's the use of talking about it? Nothing will change.

Chapter 21

Why Asking for Help is So Difficult

"Look, you can't imagine how scary it is for me. I know that if I don't get help I could die, but if I ask for help they may put me in a nursing home, and then I am sure I will die," lamented one senior, explaining why it is difficult for seniors to ask for help. There are many factors that contribute to this problem. Seniors identify embarrassment, dignity, fear, ignorance, and stubbornness as some of the factors that hold them back from asking for help. Families who take the time to understand these feelings will be in a better position to assist their older loved ones.

Embarrassment

Seniors, like all of us, want to be independent. No one wants to be perceived as needy and weak. One senior described how he did not want his family to think less of him, and therefore insisted on paying neighbors to run errands for him. The problem became a financial one, as he could not afford to pay for errands as often as he needed. He sometimes went without food or medication to avoid the embarrassment of asking for help. Sometimes an older person wants to hide the reality of his or her situation from others, not wanting others to know how bad things really are.

Dignity

Seniors often resist asking for help, saying, "I've done it this way all my life." Seniors experience a great number of transitions as they age. One of the hardest to face is the realization that they are no longer capable of managing independently. It is upsetting to families to realize that an older loved one has become dependent and vulnerable. Seniors and families sometimes equate "needing help" with "failure". Because of this, an older person will sometimes sacrifice their well-being for their dignity. The fear of losing independence and control weighs heavily on many seniors. For successful aging, seniors need to feel that they have the ability and opportunity to make choices, and that they still have input into decisions that need to be made.

Fear

"If they knew how bad things are, they'd put me away." Instead of feeling safe about asking for help with grocery shopping, refilling prescriptions, balancing a checkbook, transportation to a medical appointment, or house cleaning, seniors often shy away from asking out of fear. Some fear that if they ask for a bit of help, their families will think that 24-hour help is needed. Another fear is that they will become a burden on their family and friends. With just a little bit of support, many seniors can remain in their own homes. In 1982, 6.2% of persons over age 65 lived in nursing homes, compared to 3.4% in 1999. Today's seniors are living longer, healthier, more independent lives.

Ignorance

Seniors and their families struggle with defining what help is needed. Many seniors do not ask for help because they no longer know anyone they can ask. One senior said that she used to count on her close friends and neighbors when she needed help. Now in her nineties, she has outlived many of her friends and neighbors and no longer has a local support system to help her. Seniors often express concern that their families try hard, but don't really know how to help. Despite good intentions, families may over-promise the amount of help they can realistically give. Many families make the mistake of waiting too long to acknowledge that help is necessary to maintain the health and safety of older loved ones. When families make emergency decisions without the input of older loved ones, seniors feel resentment and adjust less easily. Many healthcare professionals like social workers, life care planners, and occupational therapists can assist with determining what services are needed and who can meet those needs.

Stubbornness

"I don't want to admit that I need help," stated one active senior. "I want to be the same person, strong and independent, that I was twenty years ago." As seniors age, the ability to shift thinking patterns and adjust to change decreases. Routines become even more important. Many seniors feel that their routines and privacy will be interrupted if help comes into the home.

Unresolved family conflicts may keep an older person from asking for help from his or her family. Seniors may express resentment that their family cannot "take care of them" and families can feel a great deal of anger and guilt about this. Many factors can contribute to a senior's stubborn determination to not ask for help, or to refuse help when it is offered.

Successful Communication Strategies

1. Respect the right of older loved ones to make decisions for themselves. Give advice, but do not manipulate situations.
2. Carefully choose the time and place for emotionally charged discussions.
3. Let your loved one know in advance what exactly you would like to discuss with him or her.

4. Begin conversations by discussing what is working in a given situation. Then, review why it is working. This approach starts the meeting positively and opens the door to creative solutions.
5. Be open-minded about several possible solutions for any problem. Limiting a discussion to only one solution can cause conflict.
6. Allow for disagreement in any discussion. Respect different viewpoints and perspectives.
7. Be aware that tone of voice and body language are powerful communication tools.
8. Stick to the agreed-upon topic of conversation.

Suggestions for Families:
1. Some disorders, such as dementia, affect a person's ability to safely judge situations and ask for appropriate help. Families may need to prepare in advance for difficult situations.
2. Families need to prepare for a broad range of reactions and responses. Planning for many different possibilities can help to avoid explosive situations.
3. Background noise can interfere with hearing and concentration. Choose a quiet, comfortable spot for a conversation.
4. Seniors often need more time to think things over. Allow the discussion to end, and then agree to reconvene for a follow-up discussion if necessary.
5. Ask a family friend, counselor, or clergy member to facilitate family meetings if necessary.
6. Outside professionals such as financial advisors or attorneys can be helpful if seniors do not want to discuss their financial situation with family.

Chapter 22

The Stress of Aging

Stress is an everyday part of life, at any age. It is the mind and body's response to life events, circumstances, and situations. The tension created by stress can actually motivate people to accomplish tasks. For example, paying a bill on time relieves the tension and worry that consequences might occur if it were not paid. Learning to cope with stress is an important strategy in aging.

Stress can be caused by issues such as not having enough time or money, experiencing pain, the death of a loved one, relocation, illness, and loneliness. The body and the emotions react differently to stress. Both reactions are caused by the release of chemicals in the body when stress is experienced.

Physical Response	Emotional Response
• Increased blood pressure • Faster breathing • Muscle tension • Upset stomach • Insomnia • Neck or back pain • Sweaty hands	• Anxiety • Nervousness • Fear • Frustration • Anger • Impatience • Impaired concentration

It is important that a doctor determine if the symptoms your loved one is experiencing are stress-related or caused by something else.

Managing Stress

Stress can be damaging to the body and the emotions. It can interfere with daily activities and relationships and can contribute to long-term health problems like chronic pain and heart disease. Stress can be managed and reduced by learning effective tools and techniques. Stress management techniques involve three aspects:

1. Recognize the symptoms of stress.
2. Remove the causes of stress.
3. Reprogram the response to stress.

Recognize the Symptoms of Stress

Listen for the Message

The body's stress reaction is designed to enhance a person's natural response to a situation. Stress sends chemicals into the bloodstream and brain to enhance performance; this is often referred to as the "fight or flight" response to emergency situations. Help an older person to recognize and journal situations in which they feel stress. Recognizing the symptoms is the first step. Use the stress checklist at the end of this chapter to identify symptoms of stress in an older person.

Find Support

Everyone feels stress. Senior support groups are ideal avenues for learning to recognize stress patterns and identify coping strategies. Many hospitals and community mental health clinics offer senior support groups that address stress. Individual counseling for older persons may also be beneficial.

Learn to Say "NO"

Setting boundaries is very difficult for many people who want to be helpful to others. Stress builds when an older person constantly feels drained and responsible for others. Teach them to recognize their limits in terms of energy and time. Help them learn to say "NO" to protect their health and well-being. People who never learn to set boundaries may experience increased physical illness or depression as stress builds. Stress not only contributes to illness, but also exacerbates it. Encourage older persons to establish balance in their day with a combination of leisure, self-care, physical, social, and work activities.

Remove the Causes of Stress

Journal Stress Patterns

By keeping a journal and tracking the patterns when stress symptoms are experienced, your older loved one may be able to come up with ways to avoid the stress reaction. For example, a person may experience stress if he or she is running 15 minutes late for a doctor's appointment; allowing extra time and leaving early could allow the stress reaction to be avoided. Look for patterns and situations that come up on a regular basis.

To Do Lists

Do. Delegate. Dump. These are the three options for handling "loose ends" that can cause stress. Many older people feel stress build as they juggle a list of items they feel they need to get done. Soon, feelings of being overwhelmed build into feelings of anxiety. Help your loved one create a list of "To Dos," then evaluate what items on the list can be done immediately. Put these on the calendar and cross them off when completed. What can be delegated? Hire a cleaning person or an organizer to assist with regular tasks. What items can be dumped from the list? If some items on the list are impossible to accomplish for lack of time or money, simply dump them from the priority list.

Environmental Factors that May Increase Stress
Environmental stressors are factors like light, noise, and air quality, which exacerbate stress by placing more demands on the body. Some factors to consider are:

- **Lighting**
  The average 80-year-old requires three times the amount of light than he or she did at age 20. Eyestrain with inadequate lighting causes stress. Sunlight helps to improve mood and provides needed illumination around the house.

- **Background Noise**
  Persons with impaired hearing frequently complain about the sound of air conditioners, refrigerators, etc. Background music also contributes to confusion and distraction for persons with hearing devices. Minimize noise by running the dishwasher during sleep hours.

- **Clutter**
  Stacks and piles of clutter around a room increase its level of chaos. Having to sort though stacks of paperwork to find important documents produces anxiety. Simplify room layout and add plenty of storage systems for everything from the kitchen pantry to the bill-writing area.

- **Floor Layout**
  Falling is a major fear for seniors. Falls can happen when a person has difficulty negotiating a room. Being able to enter and exit a room easily is a very important safety concern for seniors. Move furniture so that the traffic lanes allow for a cane or walker. Remove throw rugs from the floor, as they can make getting to the door or phone more difficult.

Reprogram the Response to Stress

While identifying and avoiding stressful situations is helpful, there are times when everyone will experience stress. Stress can be managed and reduced by the use of effective relaxation

techniques. Like any new habit, these need to be practiced
to become familiar and effective.

Suggestions for older persons include:
- **Breathing**
  Sit quietly and take in three deep breaths. Breathe in
  through the nose, as if you were smelling a rose, and
  breathe out more rapidly through the mouth, as if you
  were blowing out birthday candles on a cake.
- **Physical Activity**
  The benefits of physical activity, and its effect on mood
  and stress reduction are significant. As little as ten
  minutes of walking a day has been shown to affect
  measurable change. Not only does exercise change the
  immediate chemistry in the brain, but its effects last
  up to six hours.
- **Progressive Relaxation Technique**
  Close your eyes while sitting or lying comfortably.
  Starting with the feet and working up through the legs,
  torso, arms, neck, and face, tense, then relax, each
  muscle group.
- **Stress Relief Imagery**
  Help your older loved one imagine putting all their
  concerns into a helium balloon and releasing the string.
  Imagine the balloon rising into the sky, carrying all
  the worries and cares with it.
- **Schedule Relaxation Time**
  Structure is important when coping with change and
  stress. Encourage your older loved one to pencil in
  not only appointments on the calendar, but relaxation
  time as well.
- **Favorite Place**
  Help your older loved recreate a favorite vision in their
  mind. Call this "the favorite place." It can be a
  vacation spot they have been to, or a vision of serenity
  and peace like sitting on the beach or in a garden.
  When under stress, an older person can visualize
  "going" to their favorite place. This is especially useful
  when stuck in a shopping line or in a traffic jam.

Through the recognition of stressful conditions and situations, the removal of stressors, and the reprogramming of stress reactions, stress management can be achieved.

For more information contact:
- The local mental health clinic
- The local senior center
- Clinicians including social workers, geriatric occupational therapists, psychiatric nurses, psychologists, psychiatrists, and psychotherapists

---

Stress Checklist

Everyone experiences stress differently. Review these common symptoms of stress with your loved one.

____ Increased irritability or grouchiness.

____ Change in appetite – either an increase or decrease.

____ Increased use of alcohol to "calm down" or relax.

____ Increased tearfulness.

____ Decreased concentration.

____ Restless feelings.

____ Racing thoughts in the middle of the night.

____ Sudden feelings of panic.

____ Increased awareness of pain.

____ Change in sleep patterns – either an increase or decrease.

____ Increased desire to be alone.

____ Increased feelings of pressure to get more done.

____ Feelings of guilt.

____ Feeling overwhelmed.

____ Wanting to "get away" for a while.

____ Feeling "keyed up."

Chapter 23

Staying Busy and Feeling Needed

Free time for older persons is a relatively new idea for society. The Social Security Act of 1935 provided, for the first time in our country's history, a means for older persons to retire from employment and pursue other activities. Many seniors approach the retirement years with expectations of enjoying their increased leisure and relaxation time. Frequently, however, they are unprepared for the stresses that also accompany aging.

The senior population of the United States is changing rapidly. Life expectancy has increased by nearly 30 years since 1900, and the number of Americans over age 85 increased 38% from 1990 to 2000. Today's seniors are living more independently, and are healthier and more active than previous generations. These numbers are expected to continue to rise during the next thirty years.

Successful aging involves maintaining not only physical health, but also a sense of life's purpose, satisfaction, and well-being. Retiring from an active career can bring feelings of sadness and emptiness, even loss of identity. With the loss of social recognition and productivity that may accompany retirement, seniors often experience a decline in self-esteem. Families can assist older loved ones by encouraging seniors to continue pursuing meaningful activities in later years. When previously enjoyed activities become difficult, seniors need to find new activities that stimulate them and provide satisfaction.

Meaningful activities can meet many needs for older persons:

- Staying connected to the community.
- Providing social interaction.
- Meeting and making new friends.
- Using skills, talents, and a wealth of life experience to benefit others and feel productive and useful.
- Providing ongoing learning and mental stimulation.
- Staying physically active.
- Coping better with loss and pain.
- Providing a sense of accomplishment.

How Much is Enough

Choosing the right number of meaningful activities per week can be challenging. The "right amount" varies from person to person. Work with loved ones to achieve a balanced schedule of meaningful activities, social interaction, medical appointments, home management chores, and spiritual activities. The schedule will need to be adapted to take into account changes in weather, physical ability, mental or cognitive ability, and personal interests.

Suggestions for Families:

1. Contact local organizations such as United Way, religious organizations, soup kitchens, schools, food banks, Meals on Wheels, and homeless shelters for local volunteer opportunities.
2. Contact national organizations such as The Salvation Army, the American Red Cross, the American Heart Association, the American Cancer Society, and the Arthritis Foundation for volunteer opportunities.
3. Look in the local newspaper for posted volunteer opportunities for seniors.

4. Contact community YMCA and senior centers for special programs for older persons.
5. Many local libraries offer programs and lectures that may be of interest to your older loved one.
6. Local fitness centers and hospitals offer many fitness programs and support group options.
7. The National Senior Service Corps matches people over the age of 55 with needs in the local community.
8. State Agencies on Aging provide numerous contacts for seniors.
9. Adult day clubs provide services for seniors who need structure and supervision during the day.
10. Many community colleges and adult learning centers provide programs and classes designed to facilitate successful aging.
11. More and more intergenerational programs provide the opportunity for seniors and young people to interact and benefit from one another. One such organization is the Foster Grandparents Program.
12. Many senior housing complexes and assisted living facilities provide regular recreational activities. As an older person's health fails, in-house programs become all the more important.
13. Transportation is often a challenge. Look to the local Red Cross, senior centers, places of worship, and public transportation for assistance

Activities Checklist

Help older loved ones evaluate specific areas of interest for leisure, recreational, social, and volunteer activities.

____ **With Large Groups:** conferences, conventions, travel groups, tours, museums, parks, large organizations.

____ **With Small Groups:** church groups, board game clubs, needlecraft groups, exercise classes, hobby clubs, committee work.

____ **Alone:** gardening, knitting, mail sorting, telephone receptionist, letter writing, and collector projects.

____ **Active Work:** tour guide, exercise class, babysitting, hiking club for seniors, Elderhostel group, adult education classes.

____ **Relaxation:** tai chi, yoga, prayer or meditation group, walking club, reading, music appreciation group, expressive art group.

____ **Competitive:** seniors' swim team, golf club, bridge club, bowling league, fund-raising team, and debate team.

____ **Rewarding:** Special Olympics, United Way, American Red Cross, adult education programs, literacy volunteer, hospice volunteer.

____ **Expressive:** support group, art appreciation group, poetry class, musical club, singing group or choir, writing group.

____ **Stimulating:** political organizations, travel log presentations, reminiscing groups, memoir clubs, theater groups, reading clubs.

Section 4

Spiritual Well-Being and Aging

Chapter 24

Assisting Seniors with Spirituality

*We worry too much about something to live on, and
too little about something to live for.*
- Jimmy Townsend

*Truly I say I have no regrets.
I have no unsatisfied dreams.*
- Donald Richardson, in his last months of life
following a battle with brain cancer

Part of the aging process frequently involves a deepening sense of spirituality. Statistics show that many older persons experience a newfound sense of spirituality. Many either continue to practice or return to their earlier religious beliefs. Assisting older loved ones in nurturing their spiritual beliefs and practices is a vital role of families. People's sense of spirituality is an important factor not only in how people age, but also in how they approach the end of life.

Spirituality and Religion
Spirituality is frequently defined as being broader than religion. Persons not associated with one particular religion

can consider themselves spiritual. Spirituality is defined in the dictionary as "life and consciousness away from the body." Religion is often defined as the practical expression of spirituality; the structure, organization, and practices of belief. Different religions offer different perspectives on what eternal life is like. For many, spirituality is a *relationship* with God, rather than a religion. For others, spirituality is a sense of peace, well-being, and contentment with self, others, and the universe. Spirituality integrates all aspects of life and is often seen as a search for purpose or meaning in life. Spirituality can have an internal component (beliefs and thoughts) as well as an external component (practices and expression of beliefs). Many studies have explored the relationship between the health and happiness of older persons, and their expression of spiritual beliefs and religious practices.

Research Findings on the Religious Practices of Older Adults

- Persons who attended religious services at least once a week were 56% less likely to have been hospitalized during the previous year.
- Patients aged 60 years or older, with no religious affiliation, spent an average of 25 days in the hospital, compared with 11 days for those with some religious affiliation.
- African Americans who attended religious services more than once a week had life expectancies up to seven years longer than non-attendees.
- Daughters of women who had a strong religious commitment were 60 to 80% less likely to have experienced a major depressive episode within a ten-year period.
- Many older people report that faith assists them in coping with loss and change.

Aging from a Spiritual Perspective

- **Does religiosity increase with age and proximity to death?**
  A 25-year study conducted by the National Opinion Research Center, in which Americans self-reported on their religiosity, indicated a consistent increase in religiosity with age.
- **What age group experiences the largest increase in religiosity?**
  Greater religiosity occurs for persons during their forties and fifties, possibly correlating with the realization of one's mortality, or the death of a parent.
- **Are strongly religious persons healthier?**
  Sixty-three percent of males with excellent health report "strong" religiosity, whereas only 30% of males with fair/poor health report "strong" religiosity.

Spiritual Distress

At a time when spiritual expression and support is most vital, many seniors experience spiritual distress because they are less able to access this support. Impaired physical and mental health, lack of transportation, and immobility prevent many seniors from practicing and enhancing their spirituality.

Possible causes of spiritual distress may include the inability to maintain previous spiritual practices, loss of connection to people with similar beliefs, personal tragedy, and the inability to communicate spiritual needs. Threats to spirituality may include:

- Loss of job, abilities, or living status.
- Challenged value systems, like forced retirement.
- Separation from culture or religion due to relocation.
- Death of a significant person.
- Personal or family disaster.
- Decreased ability to function independently.
- Perceived loss of freedom or choice.
- Decreased self-esteem.

Symptoms of spiritual distress can include depression, hopelessness, feelings of abandonment, feeling separated from God or the universe, anger, isolation, and feeling lost or dissatisfied with life. Families can assist older loved ones with strategies to enhance spiritual growth and fulfillment.

Suggestions for Families
1. Use the checklist at end of this chapter to determine if spiritual distress is a concern.
2. Engage the services of clergy or a chaplain to assist in meeting unmet spiritual needs.
3. Rule out depression with the help of a medical professional.
4. Help loved ones identify ways in which they have coped with difficult situations in the past.
5. Set realistic spiritual goals like attending a prayer service once a week, or attending a faith-based senior support group.
6. Adapt previous spiritual practices to meet new needs. For example, instead of Bible-reading, acquire a set of Bible Books on Tape for persons with visual impairment.
7. Engage the services of an occupational therapist to evaluate and design a strategy for adapted spiritual expression when physical, mental, or cognitive limitations exist.
8. Determine where and when the senior feels most spiritually connected, and create a plan to enhance this opportunity.
9. Respectfully honor differing values and beliefs.
10. Encourage older persons to express their spiritual, religious, or social needs.
11. Understand the importance of personal dignity and the power of individual spiritual expression.
12. Be kind, and practice good listening skills.
13. Model an attitude of gratitude to those around you.
14. Instill hope in aging loved ones by helping them in prayer, meditation, spiritual exploration, problem-solving, and relaxation.

Spiritual Expression and Ways to Enhance Spiritual Growth
Where there is a will...there is a way. Commit to finding alternative, nurturing ways for your older loved one to grow spiritually. Consider some of these options:
- Recorded soulful music or poetry.
- Televised religious services.
- Artistic expression through collage or writing.
- Regular visits by clergy or chaplains.
- Taped worship messages.
- Personal expression through photographs and albums.
- Day trips to places of spiritual importance.
- Weekly meetings with prayer or support groups.
- Journaling of life lessons.
- Prayer partners.
- Videotaping the stories that are part of a family's heritage and culture.
- Recording a loved one's "lessons of life" conversation.
- Journaling thoughts regarding "wisdom for the next generation."
- Recorded sacred readings and meditations.
- Congregational visitation programs for comfort and encouragement.
- Homebound spiritual outreach programs.

Spirituality Checklist

Help assess an older person's level of spiritual distress by asking the following:

_____ Do you feel your life has purpose?

_____ Do you have a faith that provides comfort for you?

_____ Are you able to practice your spiritual beliefs as you would like?

_____ Would you like assistance to help nurture your spirituality?

_____ Do you feel a sense of spiritual peace and contentment?

_____ Do you wrestle with any unresolved spiritual issues?

_____ Do certain activities or practices nurture your sense of peace and contentment?

_____ What is limiting your spiritual growth?

_____ Do you feel pressured to accept spiritual beliefs that you disagree with?

_____ Are there any steps you would like to take to grow spiritually?

_____ Would you like to participate in spiritual activities on a regular basis?

Chapter 25

Attitudes For Successful Aging

The Family Challenge

Negative attitudes are one of the most difficult things that family members must contend with as a loved one ages. Many situations that were once easy to overcome now loom as large challenges for seniors. Older loved ones experience many, many areas of loss. As a result, life can no longer appear joyful or easy. Strong evidence shows that spiritual and religious beliefs can affect attitude, and a more positive, hopeful attitude contributes to successful aging.

Theories of Aging

No one knows for certain why we age the way we do. Several theories exist about the aging process, but none have been proven. Few people, however, doubt that attitude has a great deal to do with aging. For the spiritual older person, aging is often seen as a blending of the physical, psychological, and spiritual aspects of life. Many people express the belief that the end of one's physical life is the beginning of one's eternal life. Physical life, it is believed, is merely a preparation for eternal spiritual life. Successful and positive aging, then, has less to do with chronological age and physical condition, than with healthy attitudes that are developed during younger years. Listed below are some common theories of aging:

- **The Program Theory** holds that cells are pre-programmed to live for about 120 years. Regardless of what physical developments occur, cells cannot live longer than 120 years. Some seniors achieve remarkable milestones in aging, allowing them to outlive even some of their grandchildren.
- **The Wear and Tear Theory** proposes that our bodies simply wear out after a period of time. The parts break down and the body ceases to function. This theory states that aging begins in middle age, when the reality of our mortality sets in. This process, from a spiritual perspective, is normal and natural, allowing people time to accept the frailty of earthly existence and prepare for eternal life. How people experience aging varies widely, depending mostly on attitude.

Many studies have explored the benefit of thankful attitudes / spiritual practices from an aging perspective. Recent findings indicate that spiritual practices affect even blood pressure. Persons who pray or meditate daily appear to be less likely to have high blood pressure.

Dr Bernard Siegel, author of *Love, Medicine & Miracles* states that "Notable changes and reversals in disease progression are well documented. Regardless of what we believe may or may not be the vehicle for improved well-being, we arrive at a better place through prayer, meditation, or the simple process of pausing to give thanks."

Suggestions for Families
1. Help loved ones find one thing they are grateful for each day.
2. Set up a system for loved ones to record a list of blessings in a journal or on a cassette tape. Reviewing this list on a weekly basis is most effective in turning a negative attitude into a more positive one.
3. Encourage seniors to reach out to others. Frequently, older persons feel that they can no longer contribute to society, and regret being alive. By helping others,

people increase their self-esteem and feel more productive.

4. Help older persons who say "I can't do that" to find one small action they can take to move forward. Someone who is homebound may not believe they can help others, but a short phone call or note of encouragement from them can change someone's day.

5. Rule out possible depression if a significant change of attitude occurs.

6. Be aware that poorly managed or exacerbated pain can change a person's attitude significantly. Follow up with a physician as needed.

The Gratitude Tree

Donald Richardson, in his life and work, maintained an attitude of gratitude.

He shared this story with his family:

> "When I came home from work each day, before walking in the door burdened with my concerns of the day, I paused outside on my lawn in front of a favorite tree. On that tree I visualized hanging up my problems of the day, freeing me to walk into my home and the warmth of my family while leaving the cares of my workday outside." He went on to say that as he became wiser, he paused daily to reflect on what blessings he had in his life, shifting to a more positive attitude. He not only left his concerns outside on the tree, but also was able to assume an attitude of gratitude before walking into his home and the arms of the people he loved. He closed the story by saying he eventually changed the name of the tree from the Trouble Tree to the Gratitude Tree.

The Gratitude Journal

People observe only what they deliberately set out to see. For example, if a person is determined to find feathers during the day, they will notice more feathers than you can believe. The same is true with blessings. When a person decides in their mind and heart to find blessings in being alive each day, they will find them. Of course, not all days provide an abundance of blessings, so journaling a list of things to be grateful for each day helps to change attitudes about life. One senior shared that this simple daily exercise of noticing and journaling blessings helped her overcome feelings of hopelessness.

Tips About Giving Thanks

1. By giving thanks daily, people begin to find what they are grateful for. Encourage your loved one to give thanks before each meal, even if the thank you is directed to no one in particular.
2. Recognize that giving thanks is a body-wide process. While it starts in the mind when we verbalize words, each cell in the body is affected by an act of thanksgiving.
3. Thanksgiving is not limited to a belief in the existence of God. People can express thanksgiving for relationships, life, breath, medicine, nature, pets, etc.
4. Beginning the day with a time of thanksgiving can develop into a meaningful spiritual practice.
5. Asking God or the Universe or a Higher Power to intercede in daily struggles helps to change attitudes in measurable ways.
6. Developing spiritual goals and taking steps to achieve them provides a vision of hope for the future and structure for each day.
7. Keeping a diary of answered prayer provides nourishment for personal faith.

Attitude Checklist

____ Consult a physician if a sudden change of attitude is noted.

____ Family should help determine if underlying pain is present.

____ Family can assist by helping an older loved one establish meaningful goals and a rewarding daily routine.

____ Incontinence may be troubling an older person who is no longer interested in activities outside the home. Determine how to best address the problem with the help of a visiting nurse, occupational therapist, or physician.

____ Set up a daily calendar and schedule of meaningful activities for each month.

____ Include in-home, community, and social activities that provide both support and stimulation.

____ Consult a chaplain, pastor, or spiritual leader to assist with underlying spiritual issues and needs.

____ Address financial issues clearly so anxiety over money can be reduced.

____ Consider an alternative living situation if loneliness and lack of stimulation are recurring issues.

____ Plan holiday get-togethers well in advance so seniors can look forward to the family celebrations.

____ Establish an achievable way for seniors to journal blessings for each day.

Chapter 26

The Power of Prayer

Prayer changes things. "Prayer and meditation cause measurable changes in hormonal processes in the body," according to Herbert Benson, MD, president of Harvard's Mind/Body Medical Institute. These changes enhance the immune system, affecting how the body defends itself against disease. Some researchers believe that people are genetically motivated to connect with a higher power." A recent study found that the outcome of heart surgery was significantly improved when the patient had a group of people praying for him or her. Monks living lives of daily prayer and meditation at the Zen Mountain Monastery near Woodstock, NY, report the absence of any life-threatening illnesses among their population.

An article by Susan P Melia, of Assumption College, discusses the findings of Susan McFadden, a professor of psychology at the University of Wisconsin. Dr McFadden interviewed women between the ages of 65 and 98, and, in her unpublished study, identified common themes that reflect the importance of prayer for older women. For these women, prayer serves as a coping strategy, reflects a personal relationship with God, helps one to be in God's presence, helps to overcome fears, is an opportunity to express requests, and enhances a sense of gratitude.

Many older persons use prayer to deepen their relationship not only with God, but also with those around them. As persons age, their sense of making a contribution sometimes declines. Prayer allows them to reach out to others by praying for individuals, families, groups, leaders, and nations, and can effect powerful change on every level. Seniors note that the form of prayer can be as different as one person's belief is from another's. Some people start the day with a scheduled devotional routine, while others pray informally throughout the day. One senior shared the following model of prayer:

J = Jesus
O = Others
Y = You

He identified the "JOY" formula as helpful in prioritizing how he brings his requests and thoughts to God.

Seniors who pray regularly state that their prayer life is not only satisfying, but also effective in changing their outlook on life. During earlier years, many did not have as much time to pray. Now the time factor has changed for them. They state that they have more time to allow their prayers to be answered, or for God to work in their life. One senior expresses it this way, "Sometimes God's answer to prayer is a change in how I feel about what I am going through."

The time and place of prayer is individual. Some people chose to be with others of similar faith, either in a house of worship or in a home prayer meeting. Others find the presence of God in nature, reflected in the beauty around them. Still others experience prayer in the regular events that unfold in a day, when they have a feeling of companionship with God. This intimate relationship offers comfort and peace for today and for the days to come.

Prayer is a vital factor not only in managing life on earth, but also in providing hope for the future. Many believe that a strong faith reinforced by active spiritual participation may help persons cope with life stressors, particularly physical health problems later in life. In the 1997 Yankelovich Partners survey of over one thousand adults, 81 % of Americans agreed that they "believed in the existence of heaven, where people live forever with God after they die." As persons age, the hope of eternal life to end suffering becomes all the more powerful.

Statistics on Health and Prayer
In an article by Phil Vinall for CBS Health Watch, the following statistics were reported:
- Hospital patients visited by chaplains for 15 minutes daily had 29 % shorter hospital stays, and used 66 % less pain medication, compared to patients who were not visited.
- Elderly heart patients were 14 times less likely to die after surgery if they found strength or comfort in their faith, and were also socially active.
- Patients who attended religious services involving prayer at least once a week were 56 % less likely to have been hospitalized during the previous year.

Suggestions for Families
1. Support your older loved one in expressing his/her personal beliefs.
2. Honor the differences you may have in beliefs.
3. Encourage your loved one to maintain meaningful prayer routines.
4. Establish a location in your senior loved one's home that they can go to for daily meditation and reading of a devotional passage if desired. Provide enough light and a large-print version of the text as needed.
5. Talk with your loved one about his/her beliefs.
6. Establish community support with a local place of worship, so your loved one can be prayed for and visited by clergy as desired.
7. Talk about what gets in the way of being able to pray as he/she would like.
8. Assist persons with dementia and cognitive challenges to pray and to express their beliefs.

9. Provide audiotapes of prayer and worship when reading is no longer possible.
10. Know your loved one's wishes concerning the service that will celebrate their life following their passing. Find out favorite songs, hymns, prayers, and passages that they would want incorporated into the service.
11. In the presence of physical or cognitive disability, consult an occupational therapist to help loved ones express their spiritual beliefs.

Prayer Checklist
Is anything limiting the prayer life of your loved one?

____ Do they need assistance in developing a prayer routine?

____ Are their individual beliefs and practices being honored?

____ Do they have a network of like believers on which to depend?

____ Do they need any special accommodations in their meditation or prayer life, such as a large-print book?

____ Do you know the wishes of your loved one in expressing their spirituality?

____ Do you avoid imposing your beliefs on your loved one?

____ Is your loved one able to explore their spirituality as often as they'd like?

____ If a disability is interfering with spiritual expression, has an occupational therapist been consulted?

____ Are items of spiritual expression accessible to your loved one?

Chapter 27

Making Today Count

With many years behind them, older persons look back at their history and see how it has shaped them. Good memories allow people to reflect on past successes and achievements, giving a sense of meaning to their life. The future holds many unknown factors. Life is lived in the present moment.

You must live in the present, launch yourself on every wave, find your eternity in each moment. Fools stand on their island opportunities and look toward another land. There is no other land, there is no other life but this.
-Henry David Thoreau

Live with intention. Walk to the edge. Listen hard. Practice wellness. Play with abandon. Laugh. Choose with no regret. Continue to learn. Appreciate your friends. Do what you love. Live as if this is all there is.
-Mary Anne Roadacher-Hershey

Start living now. Stop saving the good china for that special occasion. Stop withholding your love until that special person materializes. Every day you are alive is a special occasion. Every minute, every breath, is a gift from God.
–Mary Manin Morrissey

Yesterday is history, tomorrow is a mystery. Today is a gift, that is why we call it The Present.
– Author Unknown

Tips for Successful Aging for Seniors and Their Families

- **Continue to Set Goals**
  Encourage older loved ones to set goals in four areas of their life: physical well-being, spiritual well-being, social well-being, and mental well-being. Goals can be set monthly or quarterly, and then broken down into weekly and daily action steps.
- **Have an Attitude of Gratitude**
  Establish a morning routine in which you review blessings. Journal ideas and insights. Give thanks for at least one person or thing each day.
- **Live Your Own Life**
  When a person is young, they worry about what others are thinking about them. In middle age, people could care less what others think. In the senior years, people come to realize that no one was ever thinking about them anyway!
- **Keep Learning**
  Never stop reaching for something to be better at.
- **Never Stop Serving Others**
  Self-esteem comes naturally when a person is proud of what they do. No matter how great or small, a thoughtful deed is always appreciated. Write a note,

make a call, smile at a stranger, or touch someone meaningfully by saying "thank you" each and every day.

- **Meditate Each Day**
  Grow spiritually each day through meditation and prayer.
- **Stay Connected with Friends and Family**
  Social relationships dramatically affect how we age. Never stop being able to make a new friend. Join a senior club or activity center that offers lots of stimulating activities for the mind and body.
- **Use it or Lose it**
  Move your body in some way every day. Stretch, walk, exercise, and stay active to feel vital every day. If necessary, consult an exercise specialist to establish an achievable, customized exercise plan.
- **Find Peace**
  Make peace with those you have wronged. Make peace with God in order to experience forgiveness and serenity each day.
- **Get a Pet**
  A pet offers unconditional love and loyalty. Pets provide incredible companionship and give you reason to get up each day. Research shows that pet owners experience longer, healthier lives.
- **Find Humor in Each Day**
  Be able to laugh at yourself. Find something to laugh about each and every day. Research confirms the health benefits of humor and laughter.

Daily Routines

Creating meaningful daily routines helps seniors cope with change and the feelings of loss that come with aging. Without a daily routine and goal, it is too easy to say, "I don't feel like getting up today." Daily goals can be as simple as calling two friends in a day. Other ideas that may help older loved ones to make the most of every day include:

- Taking a daily walk.
- Writing a note of encouragement to someone.
- Getting together with others at least three times a week.
- Taking a relaxing shower or bath.
- Going to the library.
- Having a hot lunch with friends at the Senior Center.
- Helping someone else.
- Writing a note or letter of thanks to someone.
- Building a model.
- Working on a puzzle.
- Going shopping.

Chapter 28

Relaxation Techniques for Seniors

O vercoming the stress of daily living is vital for the health and well-being of seniors. Aging brings numerous changes for most people, many of which cause feelings of stress. Stress can make people age more quickly, and aggravates many physical, emotional, and mental disorders. Stress has been found to depress the immune system, which then makes seniors more susceptible to colds and flu. Stress has also been linked to many illnesses including cancer, asthma, high blood pressure, arthritis, stomach ulcers, back pain, indigestion, and heart disease.

The Body's Response to Stress

Adrenaline enters bloodstream
Heart rate increases

Breathing becomes shallow

Blood flow changes, leaving
the skin surface and going
to internal organs and brain

Blood clots more easily, causing a dangerous situation for persons with blood vessel damage

Increased amount of hydrochloric acid is released by stomach

Muscle tension increases, creating potential for headache, pain, and muscle injury

Wasted oxygen, energy, and nutrients, and risk of long-term damage to vital organs

Relaxation Techniques to Reduce Stress

Effective relaxation decreases blood pressure, slows heart rate, releases muscle tension, reduces pain, increases the flow of oxygen, and counters the body's response to stressful situations. Relaxation techniques for seniors can include breathing, daily exercise, yoga, tai chi, meditation/prayer, progressive relaxation, and daily breaks.

Breathing
Diverse kinds of breathing affect the body differently. Encourage the use of each type of breathing as needed.
- **Deliberate Awareness Breathing** helps to calm racing thoughts and increase relaxation by focusing on the air flowing in and out, without trying to control it.

- **Deep Breathing** at a slowed pace helps to relax both the body and the mind. Start by breathing in through the nose, as if you were smelling a bouquet of flowers; feel the air filling the lower part of the lungs and pushing the stomach out. Hold for a count of two. Release the air through the mouth, as if you were blowing out birthday candles on a cake.
- **Slow Exhale Breathing** is useful for relieving tension in muscles. Breathe in rapidly for two seconds, and then slowly exhale for a count of ten. Feel the muscles gradually relax from the feet up to the head.

Daily Exercise

Daily exercise, such as stretching and walking, has been proven to help reduce stress. Exercise reduces muscle tension and fatigue. Recommend that your loved one consult a physician who can help design an appropriate daily exercise routine.

Yoga

Yoga has been proven effective in reducing stress, relieving anxiety, lowering blood pressure, and improving breathing. Yoga programs are available in almost every town or urban area, and are frequently offered at fitness centers, wellness centers, senior centers, YMCAs, and community centers. Many yoga programs are graded by difficulty and ability level into classes such as Beginner, Intermediate, or Advanced. Many centers offer yoga programs that are adapted for persons with limitations or disabilities.

Tai Chi

Tai chi has gained popularity among seniors in America in recent years. Referred to as "the art of slowing down," tai chi is an exercise system that combines slow, graceful motions with regular, calm breathing. Movements are controlled and natural. Posture and breathing are deliberately different from the frantic pace of a stressful lifestyle. Many senior tai chi programs are available throughout the country, and through different organizations including senior centers, rest homes, nursing homes, and fitness/wellness centers.

Meditation/Prayer

Meditation and prayer have been shown to cause measurable changes in hormonal processes in the body. The soul and the body are powerfully connected. Meditation and prayer can be helpful for seniors affected by chronic illness, as well as stress-related disorders such as pain, stomach ulcers, and headaches. Meditation and prayer help slow the rate of breathing, while increasing blood flow to the brain.

Some meditation and prayer is accomplished while quietly sitting. Focus can be on a specific thought, or on nothing at all – a clearing of the mind of all worry and thoughts. Meditation and prayer can also be done in combination with movement, such as hiking in nature, or in Chinese meditative rhythms such as tai chi.

Progressive Relaxation

This effective technique can bring about a deep state of relaxation. First tensing and then relaxing a muscle can bring about blood flow changes. Starting with the neck and face, people are taught to tense (for one to two seconds) then relax their muscles. Moving from the face and neck, seniors are taught to then contract and relax muscles in the arms, chest, abdomen, hips, thighs, calves, and feet. After several repetitions, the body is very relaxed. This is an ideal technique to do before bedtime.

Daily Breaks

Routines can become monotonous and stressful. Regular breaks from a routine or chore can help relieve tension and stress. Listed below are some five-minute stress relievers:
- Take a walk outside.
- Stretch the muscles in the neck and shoulders.
- Read a poem.
- Interact with a favorite pet.
- Listen to a favorite piece of music.

- Call a friend on the telephone.
- Enjoy a cup of herbal tea or decaffeinated coffee.
- Enjoy a healthy snack.
- Write a note of encouragement to someone.
- Visualize yourself at a favorite vacation spot.

Relaxation Checklist

Help your older loved one increase relaxation by encouraging them to do any of the following:

____   Eliminate caffeine from daily diet.

____   Limit use of medications unless prescribed by a physician.

____   Avoid using alcohol to assist in relaxation.

____   Maintain a daily exercise routine.

____   Eat regular, well-balanced meals each day.

____   Go to bed and wake up at the same times each day.

____   Use relaxing background sounds, like calming music, to drown out disturbing noise.

____   Use lotions and soaps with a soothing fragrance.

____   Be realistic in setting daily goals.

____   Include leisure time in every day.

____   Keep "To Do" lists on paper to help clear the mind.

____   Laugh at least twice a day.

____   Plan time wisely by arriving early for appointments.

____   Use daily meditation and prayer.

____   Try using breathing techniques when standing in line.

____   Delegate energy-draining tasks to others.

____   Elevate feet when sitting for a period of time.

____   Don't wait to accomplish tasks at the last minute.

____   Keep favorite reading material close at hand.

Chapter 29

Using Humor to Feel Better

What soap is to the body, laughter is to the soul
- Jewish Proverb

Humor is mankind's greatest blessing
- Mark Twain

Aging brings change and increased feelings of uncertainty. One of the most enjoyable coping strategies to counter unsettling feelings is the use of humor. Humor makes the mind more adaptable, allowing it to solve problems and cope in new and better ways.

Improved Health

Humor brings about changes in the body. Numerous studies document how humor helps people cope with illness and promotes healing.

- Mood changes include: increased smiling, and increased expressions of joy, pleasure, and creativity.
- Physical changes include: increased blood flow to internal organs, release of muscle tension, positive changes in heart rate and blood pressure, release of endorphins which help manage pain, and increased immune response.

- Emotional changes include: brighter outlook on life, increased motivation and determination, more pleasant memories surface, increased sense of well-being, reduced worry and emotional tension, and increased ability to solve problems.

Many hospitals include humor channels or humor programs for their patients. Groucho Marx said, "A clown is like an aspirin; only it works twice as fast." Clare Buie Chaney says, "Laughter is like free Prozac. Humor can be the best way to relieve stress, a major factor in the onset of heart disease. In addition, laughter increases your concentration, your well-being, and your awareness, and decreases your anger levels and can aid in digestion and circulation." Humor continues to be studied for its effects on healing and wellness.

Using Humor to Solve Problems

Most people never develop the ability to solve difficult problems well; instead, they simply label situations as "hopeless" or "bad." The left side of the brain is responsible for this labeling process, which is helpful when a situation is dangerous and a quick response is needed. However, the left brain does a poor job of solving problems, because it does not think creatively. The right brain, on the other hand, is extraordinary at both humor and problem solving when given the freedom to do so. Try the following techniques:

- **Label it Differently** is a process that shifts the way we judge ourselves. For instance, when arriving at a social gathering later than expected, see yourself as "fashionably late" rather than as an idiot! When lost while driving, label yourself as enjoying a scenic drive!
- **Look for the Humor Around You**
  Here are a few real-life advertisements from the newspaper:
  - Used Cars: "Why go elsewhere to be cheated? Come here first!"
  - "Girl wanted to assist magician in cutting-off-head illusion. Blue Cross and salary offered."

- "We will oil your sewing machine and adjust tension in your home for $1.00."
- "For Rent: 6-room hated apartment."
- "We build bodies that last a lifetime."
- "Man wanted to work in dynamite factory. Must be willing to travel."
- Auto Repair Service: "Free pick-up and delivery. Try us once; you'll never go anywhere again."

Richard Lederer has collected and published church bulletin announcements in his series of books called *Anguished English, More Anguished English and Fractured English.* Included in his books:

- "Bertha Belch, a missionary from Africa, will be speaking tonight at Calvary Memorial Church in Racine. Come tonight and hear Bertha Belch all the way from Africa."
- Announcement in the church bulletin for a National PRAYER & FASTING conference: "The cost for attending the Fasting and Prayer conference includes meals."
- "Our youth basketball team is back in action Wednesday at 8 pm in the recreation hall. Come out and watch us kill Christ the King."
- "Miss Charlene Mason sang 'I will not pass this way again,' giving obvious pleasure to the congregation."
- "Ladies, don't forget the rummage sale. It's a chance to get rid of those things not worth keeping around the house. Don't forget your husbands."
- "Next Sunday is the family hayride and bonfire at the Fowlers'. Bring your own hot dogs and guns."
- "The peacemaking meeting scheduled for today has been canceled due to conflict."
- "The sermon this morning: 'Jesus Walks on the Water.' The sermon tonight: 'Searching for Jesus.'"
- "Next Thursday there will be tryouts for the choir. They need all the help they can get."

- "Barbara remains in the hospital and needs blood donors for more transfusions. She is also having trouble sleeping and requests tapes of Pastor Jack's sermons."

Smile Until Your Brain Catches Up

By intentionally holding facial muscles in the position of a smile, the brain can be triggered to release chemicals that contribute to good feelings. The brain equates a smile with pleasurable memories, which can help shift a person's mood.
- Humor For Seniors

In response to the growing need to help seniors overcome loss and manage change, humor programs are flourishing across the country. Known as Laughter Clubs, these specialized programs offer laughter exercises for seniors at every level of functioning. Certified Laughter Leaders come from many professional backgrounds, including recreational therapists, nurses, teachers, counselors, and physicians. Local programs can be found at senior centers, nursing homes, retirement communities, adult day care centers, and assisted living facilities.

Laughter Clubs offer the following advantages:
- Led by health care facilitators, the clubs can be adapted to any level of functioning and ability.
- Participants benefit from the sensory and motor stimulation offered during the program exercises.
- The club meetings are social events for older persons.
- No level of comic ability is required.
- Positive shifts in self-esteem and attitude benefit both the individual and the facility as a whole.
- Participants report an increased ability to manage daily stress.

Suggestions for Families

1. Collect tapes of favorite comedy shows like "I Love
   Lucy." Use them to help relieve tension and shift to a
   more positive attitude.
2. Collect favorite cartoons. Work with seniors in putting
   together a "Laugh Book" with pasted-in cartoons and
   jokes.
3. Purchase recorded humor tapes or make your own
   with your loved one.
4. Contact 1-800-NOW-LAFF for more information about
   North American Laughter Clubs.

Chapter **30**

Problem-Solving Skills For Seniors and Their Families

A ging brings adjustment, transitions, and frequent change. At a time in life when established routines are comfortable, many seniors are asked to make adjustments including relocating, discontinuing driving and finding alternative modes of transportation, making new friends, becoming more dependent on others, and learning to ask for help. Any one of these challenges is monumental, and several at once can seem insurmountable at times.

Frequently, problems arise when adult children see their older loved ones make decisions that seem unsafe. With their loved one's best interests in mind, they begin to assert themselves and try to deal with the situation. Older loved ones perceive that they are being judged as incompetent. What follows is hurt feelings, frustration on both sides, unresolved concerns, and a breakdown in communication.

There is a better way. Problem-solving techniques can follow several models. Two models in particular help solve issues while eliminating unnecessary conflict.

Five Question Framework
Kurt Wright, in his book *Breaking the Rules, Removing the Obstacles to Effortless High Performance,* outlines his Five Question Framework for problem-solving. He approaches

each challenge and situation from the perspective that instead of starting with the question, "What is Wrong?", solutions are best identified by asking the question, "What is Right?" His model looks like this:

Step One: **Identify the Situation / Problem / Concern**
Step Two: **What do I know is already RIGHT about this situation?**
   - What is working?
   - What is going well?
   - This is the "agenda-setting" question.
Step Three: **What is it that makes it RIGHT?**
   - Why does this feel good?
   - Why does it feel right?
   - This is the "energy-generating" question.
Step Four: **What would be ideally RIGHT?**
   - What is the ideal in this situation?
   - What would be the absolute best?
   - What would leave me with a feeling of relief, joy, or delight?
   - This is the "vision-building" question.
Step Five: **What isn't quite RIGHT yet?**
   - Start brainstorming what would make the situation better.
   - What would make the situation ideal?
   - What still needs to be tweaked?
   - This is the "gap-defining" question.
Step Six: **What resources can I find to make it RIGHT?**
   - What would get me closer to the ideal?
   - Wouldn't it be great if we could…?
   - Wouldn't it be incredible if we had…?
   - Having _____would all but eliminate the problem.
   - This is the "action-engaging" question.

Problem Solving Funnel™

Step One: **Identify the Problem**
Include who is affected by the problem.
Rate the level of concern from one to five. (one = low / five = high)
Identify how long the problem has existed.

Step Two: **Brainstorm all the Options**
Brainstorming is the process of listing all the alternatives or possible solutions to the problem. Do not attach judgment to or evaluate the possible options, just list them. Everything that is mentioned by participants can be considered an option, no matter how unreasonable it sounds.

Step Three: **Weigh Each Option**
Evaluate on paper and out loud the pros and cons of each and every option. Weigh the cost, time, energy, resources, and reasonableness of each option.

Step Four: **Choose the Three Best Options**
Rank all the options from "one to …". Choose the top three options.

Step Five: **Decide on One Option**
Identify the best option of the three remaining. Then, decide what action could be taken to initiate the plan.

Problem Solving Funnel™ Worksheet

Step One: **Identify the Problem**

Step Two: **Brainstorm all the options**

1	2
3	4
5	6
7	8
9	10

Step Three: **Weigh Each Option**

Option	Pros	Cons
1		
2		
3		
4		
5		

Step Four: **Choose the Three best options**

#1
#2
#3

Step Five: **Decide on one option**

_____

Action Step to initiate option/ solution

_____

Problem-Solving Checklist

Prepare for problem-solving discussions using the following checklist:

____ Schedule problem-solving sessions in advance to give everyone involved time to think and prepare.

____ Clearly state the issue, concern, or problem.

____ Don't allow other arguments or concerns to get the discussion off-track.

____ Use the help of a neutral party if necessary.

____ Keep your tone of voice neutral, without judgment or anger.

____ Come with an attitude of compromise.

____ Listen carefully.

____ Use "I" statements, not "you" statements. For example, "*I* feel sad," instead of "*you* make me feel sad."

____ Speak openly and freely but without a condescending or threatening tone.

____ Evaluate who is at risk in the current situation.

____ Consider options that have yet to be identified or discussed.

____ Agree that problem-solving is not about winning or losing.

____ Watch for body language while you are speaking and listening.

____ Be willing to "agree to disagree" until a later time.

____ Establish what problem-solving model will be used and stick with it.

Chapter **31**

Tips to Create a Memoir and Leave a Legacy

The tools people use to adjust to aging have probably been with them throughout their lives. The past, with all its challenges and achievements, makes people what they are in the present. People approach aging with the character traits and strengths that served them in years past; the challenges of aging today are new, but not without similarities to challenges that have already been overcome. Looking back into the past allows good memories to bring a sense of well-being and confidence to seniors.

Memoir work is the process of looking back into one's life. It is a process of reflection, celebration, and healing. Reflecting on the wisdom gained, celebrating the achievements, and seeking peace and closure for those wrongs that can be made right, is a powerful process for all.

What Can Be Achieved by Putting Together a Memoir?
A memoir, regardless of form, becomes a treasured legacy that can be passed down for generations. It is a marvelous coping strategy to help counter the feelings of sadness or anxiety that many older persons experience. A memoir is a gift of the heart that identifies the life activities, experiences, relationships, and roles that have occupied our lives in meaningful ways.

When Should a Memoir Project Be Done?

Many seniors wait and wait, never getting around to creating a memoir. It is not necessarily an activity to be put off until later. Any life milestone, like the birth of a grandchild, might be the perfect time to design and create a memoir. Memoirs can also be written when we want to leave a part of our story with the people we love. This often happens as seniors reflect on their life successes and many experiences.

Who Should Create a Memoir?

Memoirs can be created individually or as family projects. An individual might reflect on the key moments in their life, like milestones and treasured stories that have been repeated over the years and have become part of the family tradition. Memoirs can also reflect lessons that have been learned in life.

A family might assist a senior in planning and creating a memoir, based on what they would cherish in the years to come. About ten days before my father passed away from brain cancer, he was able to record four meaningful stories that keep his memory near to us. Hearing his voice and humor, even in his last days, is a blessing to all of us. Memoirs can vary in form. Some families may like a recording of the loved one telling a life story, while others might like a written chronology of a loved one's life events.

Are There Any Fears about a Memoir Project?

Seniors often fear that a memoir project may be a daunting task. They ask, "How can I possibly sum up my life in one book, tape, etc.?" The key is to keep it simple. Something small and meaningful is far better than an unfinished project. Start with an outline of the project. Then, create a plan involving achievable steps that can be measured along the way. Get professional help whenever needed to assist in overcoming roadblocks in the project. Occupational therapists address the mental and physical well-being of an aging person, working with the person to deal with physical and emotional challenges that can limit quality of life They are trained to overcome barriers that may make memoir work difficult.

A second fear that seniors may experience is the fear that their life may not have been the success they would have hoped. They may wonder, "Was I successful in my life? Did I accomplish what I wanted to? Was my life meaningful to others?" These are natural thoughts as people reflect on their life. The beauty of a memoir project is that one realizes that the true meaning in life is in how we have touched others, how we have been touched by others, how we have done a little good in this world, and how our life reflects the stories and events that make us who we are today. The person described in a memoir is the person that generations to come will want to know and remember.

What Types of Memoirs Are There?

Memoirs can take any form. Written memoirs include journals, letters, manuscripts, and poetry, reflecting one's life by following a chronological timeline or by answering questions like "What lessons have I learned in life?"

Audiotapes are one of the easiest memoirs to complete; they are powerful yet inexpensive. The recorded voice of a loved one is a tremendous gift.

Videotapes are a bit more complicated, but extremely effective with both the visual and auditory components. One could either be asked questions in an interview format or record photographs with segments of narration in between. For example, a picture of a first home might be on the screen as the camera records the voice of an older person telling a meaningful story about the house. Use videotape to record a person recalling the history of specific personal items that are meaningful to them, like collections of heirloom teacups, the story of a baseball caught at Yankee Stadium, or the history of the family Bible.

Visual memoirs can be objects, a photo album, or a collage of photos. Quilts and handmade items are cherished visual memoirs. Photo albums should be clearly labeled and organized sequentially in a way that tells a story. Collages can be professionally framed and reproduced.

Suggestions for Families

1. Hire the services of a personal historian if you want a professional product.
2. Enjoy the steps and challenges in completing a memoir project with your older loved one. Make it fun and meaningful.
3. Don't delay. Time is precious and the future is uncertain.
4. Use an occupational therapist to help overcome the challenges of limited hearing or sight.
5. Take the time to hire a professional photographer for family events and get-togethers.
6. Talk about life and life lessons with your older loved one. The process of talking about these issues enhances self-esteem.
7. Enjoy one another's company while you have each other.
8. Start now. A small but meaningful memoir will be a treasured legacy for your family. Break the project into small, achievable steps.
9. Enjoy the rich process of reminiscing and reflecting on how meaningful experiences and activities tell a life story.

References

Section 1:
Physical Well-Being and Aging

Anderson JV, Palombo RD, Earl R. Position of the American
    Dietetic Association; The role of nutrition in health
    promotion and disease prevention programs. *Journal of
    the American Dietetic Association.* 1998;98(2);205-208.

Ash, D. and Werlinger, C. *Exercises for Health Promotion.*
    Gathersburg, MD: Aspen Publishers, Inc. 1997.

Avers, D. Osteoporosis. *Orthopedic Physical Therapy
    Clinics of North America* (entire journal dedicated to
    prevention and treatment of osteoporosis). 1998;7:117-
    307

Barim, C. *Addressing the Needs of the Cognitively Impaired
    Elderly From a Family Policy Perspective.* The American
    Journal of Occupational Therapy. 1991;45(7):594-606.

Bicknell EH, Pike MR. Glenridge: A partnership for
    eldercare. *Journal of Community Health Nursing.*
    1993;10:97-103.

Burbank PM, Padula CA, Nigg CR. Changing health
    behaviors of older adults. *Journal of Gerontoglogical
    Nursing.* 2000;26:26-33.

Chernoff R. *Geriatric Nutrition; The Health Professional's
    Handbook.* Gaithersburg, MD: Aspend Publishers,
    Inc.; 1991.

Davolt S. New niches in physical fitness. *Physical Therapy
    Magazine.* 1997; March:32-41.

Dyck I. Health promotion, occupational therapy and multiculturalism: Lessons from research. *Canadian Journal of Occupational Therapy.* 1993;60:120-129.

Ellingson T, Conn VS. Exercise and quality of life in elderly individuals. *Journal of Gerontological Nursing.* 2000;26:17-25.

Grove NC, Spier E. Motivating the well elderly to exercise. *Journal of Community Health Nursing.* 1999; 16(3):179-189.

Haber D. *Health Promotion and Aging.* New York, NY: Springer Publishing Co.; 1994.

Harris S. Suominen H, Era P et al., ed. *Toward Healthy Aging-International Perspectives. Park I, Physiological and Biomedical Aspects. Physical Activity, Aging and Sports.* Albany, NY: Center for Study on Aging; 1994.

Hasselkans, BR. *Ethical Dilemmas in Family Caregiving for the Elderly: Implications for Occupational Therapy.* American Journal of Occupational Therapy. 1991;45(3):201-212.

Healthy People 2000: National Health Promotion and Disease Prevention Objectives (1991). Stock No. 017-001-00474-0. Government Publication Office: (202)512-1800.

Jackson J, Carlson M, Mandel D, Zemka R, Clark F. Occupation in lifestyle redesign: The well elderly study occupational therapy program. *The American Journal of Occupational Therapy.* 1998;52(5):326-335.

Koehler KM, Pareo-Tubbeh SL, Romero LJ, Baumgartner RN, Garry PJ. Folate nutrition and older adults: Challenges and opportunities. *Journal of the American Dietetic Association.* 1997;97(2):167-172.

Kutner NG, Ory MG, Baker DI, et al. Measuring the quality of life of the elderly in health promotion intervention clinical trails. *Public Health Reports.* 1992; 107:530-539.

Lewis CB. *Aging; The Healthcare Challenge.* Philadelphia: FA Davis Co.; 1985.

Lewis, SL. *Elder Care in Occupational Therapy.* Thorofare, NJ; Spack Incorporated; 1989.

O'Donnell MP. Definition of health promotion: Part III: Expanding the definition. *American Journal of Health Promotion.* 1989:3:5.

Resnick B. Spellbring AM. Understanding what motivates older adults to exercise. *Journal of Gerontological Nursing.* 2000;26;34-42.

Rothman, J. and Levine, R. Prevention Practice: Strategies for Physical Therapy and Occupational Therapy. Philadelphia, PA: W.B. Saunders Co.; 1992.

Saxon SV, Etten MJ. *Physical Change and Aging.* New York, NY: The Tiresias Press, Inc.; 1994.

Schlenker, E. *Nutrition and Aging.* Boston, MA: WCB McGraw-Hill; 1998.

Schlenker ED. *Nutrition in Aging.* 3rd ed. Boston, MA; McGraw-Hill; 1998.

Schoenfelder DP. A fall prevention program for elderly individuals. Exercise in long-term care settings. *Journal of Gerontological Nursing.* 2000;26:43-51.

Shepard RJ. *Physical Activity and Aging.* 2nd ed. Rockville, Md: Aspen Publishers Inc.;1997.

Teague, McGee; Rosenthal & Herns. *Health Promotion; Achieving High-level Wellness in the Later Years.* Madison, WI: Brown & Benchmark Publishers; 1997.

Van Norman KA. *Exercise Programming for Older Adults.* Champaign, IL: Human Kinetics; 1995.

Tinetti ME, Baker DI, McAvay G, et al. A multifactorial intervention to reduce the risk of falling among elderly living in the community. *New England Journal of Medicine. 1994;331:821-827.*

Section 2:
Mental Well-Being and Aging

About Dementia. South Deerfield: Chaning L. Bete Company, 1992.

Aldridge, S. "High Tech Memory Help." *HealthandAge.com.* 2001.
www.healthandage.comHome?gm = 20&gc = 3&1 = 1&gid1 = 244&fa = 1&path = null&x = 44&y =

Aldridge, S. "Never Too Late for Exercise." *HealthandAge.com.* 2001. 2 September 2001.
www.healthandage.com/
Home?gm = 14&gc = 2&gid1 = 510&fa = 1&path = null&x = 49&y = 10

Aldridge, S. *Stress, Vitamin E and Alzheimer's.* 3 September 2001.
www.orthop.Washington.edu/arthritis/living/stress. September 18,1998.

Barney, K.F. "From Ellis Island to Assisted Living: Meeting the Needs of Older Adults From Diverse Cultures". *American Journal of Occupational Therapy*. July 1991, Volume 5, Number 7.

Baum, C.M. "Addressing the Needs of the Cognitively Impaired Elderly From a Family Policy Perspective." *American Journal of Occupational Therapy*. July 1991, Volume 45, Number 7.

Bayles, K and Kaszniak, A.W. *Communication and Cognition in Normal Aging And Dementia*. Boston: Little Brown, 1987.

Beylin, G.E. et al. "Learning enhances adult neurogensesis in the hippocampal formation. *"Nature Neuroscience"*, 2, 203-205. 1999.

Christensen, H. "The association between mental, social and physical activity and cognitive performance in young and old subjects." *Age, Ageing*, 22, 175-182. 1993.

Davis, L.J. and Kirkland, M. *The Role of Occupational Therapy With The Elderly*. Rockville, Maryland: The American Occupational Therapy Association Inc., 1986.

Decker, M.C. "Evaluating the Client With Dementia." *Mental Health*. December 1996, Volume 19, Number 4.

Finch, C.E. "Genetics of Aging." *Science*. 278, 407-411. 1997.

Galasko, D. Clinical milestones in patients with AD followed over three years." *Neurology*, 45, 1451-1455. 1995.

Hasselkus, B.R. "Ethical Dilemmas in Family Care giving for the Elderly: Implications for Occupational Therapy". *American Journal of Occupational Therapy.* March 1991,Volume 5, Number 3.

Hayflick, L. *How and Why We Age.* Ballantine Books. 1995.

Katz, L.C. and Rubin, M. "Nuerobics Is a Unique New System of Brain Exercises." *Keeping Your Brain Alive.* www.keepyourbrainalive.com/explain.html

Katz, L.C. and Rubin, M. *Recent Findings on Memory Issues.* www.healthandage.com/html/min/ memoryzine/content/recent.htm

Knopman, D. "Atherosclerosis Risk In Communities." *MindAlert.* January 2001. 3 November 2001. http:// www.asaging.org/mindalert/ search.cfm?ID = 71&do = detail

Knopman, D."Brain Facts." *Science Information.* 2001. 13 November 2001. http://www.dana.org/brainweek/science1.cfm

Kubin, L. "Memory and Aging." August 1997. www.ext.colostate.edu/pubs/columnha/ha9703.htm

McEwen, B "Protective and damaging effects of stress mediators." *New England Journal of Medicine.* 333, 171-179. 1998.

"Memory." *Health and Age.com.* www.healthandage.com/ Home?gm = 20&gc = 3&gid21 = 14&fa = 1&path = null&x = 71&y = 5

"Mental Fitness Research." *MindAlert.* www.asaging.org/ mindalert/fitness.html

Nussbaum, P. D. *Handbook of Neuropsychology and Aging.* New York: Plenum Press. 1997.

Nussbaum, P.D. "Normal Aging." *Aging Brain, Aging Mind.* Fall 2001.

Nussbaum, P.D. "Cognitive decline in elderly depressed: A follow up Study. *The Clinical Neuropsychologist.* 9. 101-108. 1995.

Paolisso, G. et al "Oxidative stress and advancing age: Results in healthy centenarians," *JAGS*, 46, 833-838.

"Psychologists Identify Factors Associated With Cognitive Decline In Old Age." *American Psychological Association.* 1996. 13 November 2001. http://www.apa.org/releases/aging.html

Reisberg, B. "Dementia: A Systematic Approach to Identifying Reversible Causes." *Geriatrics.* April 1986, Volume 41, Number 4.

Roses, A.D. "AD: the genetics of risk." *Hospital Practice.* 32, 51-75. 1997.

Sapolsky, R.M. "Why stress is bad for your brain." *Science.* 273, 749-750. 1996.

Schmand, B. et al. "Low education is a genuine risk factor for accelerated memory decline and dementia." *Journal of Clinical Epidemiology*, 50, 1025-1033, 1997.

Tangley, L. "Aging Brains need Fresh Challenge To Stay Agile." *U.S. News.* June 5, 2001. 4 September 2001. http://n112.newsbank..../
Archives?p_action=doc&p_docid=0ED7CF67ECCD405F&p_docnum= >

Tangley, L "Eating Right May Reduce Your Risk For Alzheimer's Disease." *NeuroVista*. October/November 2000 Edition. 13 November 2001. < http:// www.aan.com/neurovista/octnov2000/ article392.html >

U.S. Department of Health and Human Services. *Mental Health: A Report of The Surgeon General*. Rockville, Maryland: U.S. Department of Health and Human Services, 1999.

Section 3:
Emotional Well-Being and Aging

Bearon, L.B. *Successful Aging: What does the "good life" look like?* 13 November 2001. http:// www.ces.ncsuedu/depts./fcs/pub/aging.htm

Blazer, D. Depression in Late Life. *Second Edition*. St. Louis: Mosby. 1993.

Brandt, A.L. *Transition Issues for the Elderly and Their Families*. 2000. 19 November 2001. http://www.ec-online.net/Knowledge/Articles/ brandttransitions.html

"Chemical Dependency and the Elderly." *Connecticut Clearinghouse*.

Crews, Fulton T. "Factors Predisposing to Alcohol and Medication Abuse in the Elderly."

Czillinger, K. *CareNotes*. "When Someone You Love is Suffering." St. Meinrad: Abbey Press, 1989.

Czillinger, K. *Depression In Later Life*. South Deerfield: Channing L. Bete Company Inc., 1999.

Edinberg, M. *The Do's and Don'ts of Communicating With Aging Patients*. 2000. 19 November 2001. http://www.ec-online.net/Knowledge/Articles/dosndonts.html.

Edinberg, M. *Family Issues*. 2000. 19 November 2001. http://www.ec-online.net/Knowledge/Articles/familyissues.html.

Financial Caregiving. 1998. 19 November 2001. http://www.ec-online.net/Knowledge/Articles/fincare.html

Foreman, J. "Alcoholism: No Refuge in Old Age." *The Boston Globe*. 20 December 1993.

Foreman, "Memo to: Older Americans Re: Preventing Alcohol Problems." Connecticut Clearinghouse.

Glass, T.A. *"Change In Productive Activity in Late Adulthood: MacAurthur Studies Of Successful Aging."* Journal of Gerontology: Social Sciences. 1995; 50(2): S65-S76.

Harrison, P. "Treating the Elderly." *The Journal*. 1996.

Hersch, G. "Leisure and Aging." *Physical and Occupational Therapy in Geriatrics*. 1990; 9(2): 55-73.

Kenny, J.A. *CareNotes*. "Wondering What's Best for an Aging Parent." St. Meinrad: Abbey Press, 1988.

King, R. *Volunteerism and Successful Aging.* March 28, 1996. 13 November2001. http://otpt.ups.edu/Gerontological_Resources? Gerontology_Manual/King-R.html

Lewis, C.B. *Aging: The Healthcare Challenge.* Philadelphia: FA Davis Co, 1985.

Lewis, S.C. Elder Care in Occupational Therapy. Thorofare: SLACK Inc., 1989.

National Senior Service Corps brochure. Washington D.C.: The Corporation for National Service.

Park, D.C. "The Aging Mind." *Fathom.* 2001. 13 November 2001. http://www.fathom.com/story/ story_printable.jhtml?storyId = 122249

Park, D.C. "Older Adults' Health and Age Related Changes: Reality Versus Myth." *American Psychology Association.* April 1988.

Rayl, A.J.S. "Attitude Plays Critical Role in Aging." *USA Today: Health.* May 3, 2000. 4 November 2001. http:// www.usatoday.com/life/health/doctor/lhdoc143.htm

Sapolsky, R. M. Why Zebras Don't Get Ulcers. New York: W. H. Freeman. 1993

Swaab, D.F. "Brain Aging and Alzheimer's' Disease, 'wear and tear' versus 'use it Or lose it'." *Neurobiology of Aging.* 1991; 12(4): 317-324.

Swaab, D.F. "Alcohol Abuse is Nothing to Wink At." *The Addiction Letter.* 1995. "Chemical Dependency and the Elderly." *Connecticut Clearinghouse.*

Section 4:
Spiritual Well-Being and Aging

(Author's Name omitted by Request). *Relaxation Techniques for Working Women*. 2001, 3 November 2001. http://ms.essortment.com/ relaxationthe_and.htm

Becker, Arthur H. *Ministry with older persons: a guide for clergy and congregations*. Minneapolis, MN: Augsburg, 1986. 221p.

Bhaerman, Steve. *Laughter and Mental Flexibiilty*. Associaiton for Applied and Therapeutic Humor. July 2001. 11 November 2001. http://www.aath.org/ art_bhaerman01.html

Bianchi, Eugene. *Aging as a spiritual journey*. New York, Crossroad, 1982. 274p.

Blazer, D. (1991). *Spirituality and Aging Well*. Generations, xv(1) pp. 61-66.

Chatters, Linda M., Jeffrey S. Levin and Robert J. Taylor. 1992 *"Antecedents and dimensions of Religious Involvement Among Older Black Adults."* Journal of Gerontology: Social Sciences 47: S269-S278.

Clingan, Donald F. 1995. *"Aging: Gathering a Spiritual Perspective."* Center for Aging Religion & Spirituality CHRONICLE. http://www.luthersem.edu/cars/ newsletters/FRSTNEWS.HTM

Clements, William C. *Ministry with the aging*. New York, NY:Haworth, 1989. 274p.

Ebersole, P., and P. Hess (1995). Toward Healthly Aging: Human Needs and Nursing Response. (5th edition) St. Louis, MO: Nosby-Year Book, Inc.

Ellor, James W. 1995. *"Special White House Conference Edition. Mini Conference Resolutions."* Center for Aging Religion & Spirtuality CHRONICLE. http://www.LUTHERSEM.EDU/CARS/NEWSLETTERS/frstnews.htm

Erikson, Erik H. *Identity and the life cycle.* New York, NY: International Universitites Press, 1959. 171p.

Falcon, Mike. *Thankful Thoughts Make Health Sense.* USA Today. 22 November 2000, Information Access: 4 November 2001. http://www.trinity.edu/~ mkearl/ger-relg.html.

Fischer, Kathleen R. *Autumn Gospel: Women in the Second Half of Life.* Mahwah, NJ: Paulist, 1995. 185p.

Fischer, Kathleen R. *Winter Grace: Spirituality for the Later Years.* Mahwah, NJ: Paulist Press, 1985. 170p.

Frankl, Viktor E. *Man's Search for Meaning: an Introduction to Logotherapy.* Boston: Beacon Press, 1992. 196p.

Griffin, Richard. *Enlightenment Through Losses and Limits: Spirituality and Disabilitiy.* Aging and Spirituality. Winter 1998. 3 September 2001. http://www.asaging.org/networks/forsa/a&s-104.html.

Hiltner, Seward. *Toward a Theology of Aging.* New York, NY: Human Sciences Press, 1975. 181p.

Hulme, William E. *Vintage Years: Growing Older with Meaning and Hope.* Philadelphia: Westminster, 1986. 120p.

Iris, Madelyn. *Retrieving Spiritual Traditions for the Elderly.* Aging & Spirituality. Summer 1999. 3 September 2001. http://www.asaging.org/networks/forsa/a&s-112.html.

Jewel, Albert, ed. *Spirituality and Ageing.* London: Kingsley, 1999. 191 p.

Kaufman, Sharon R. *The Ageless Self: Sources of Meaning in Late Life.* Madison: University of Wisconsin, 1986. 209 p.

Kimble, Melvin A. *Aging, Spirituality, and religion: a Handbook.* Minneapolis: Fortress Press, 1995. 637 p.

Kirkland, Kevin H., and Howard McIlveen. *Full Circle: Spiritual Therapy for the Elderly.* New York, NY: Haworth, 1999. 236 p.

Koch, K. (1977). *I Never Told Anybody.* New York, NY: Random House.

Koenig, Harold G. *Aging and God: Spiritual Pathways to Mental Health and Midlife and Later Years.* New York: Haworth, 1994. 544p.

Koenig, Harold G. and David B. Larson. *"Use of Hospital Services, Religious Attendance, and Religious Affiliation."* Southern Medical Journal. Vol. 91, No. 10 (1998). Pp. 925-932.

Koenig, Harold G. *Research on Religion and Aging: an Annotated Bibliography.* New York: Tarcher/Putnam, 1997. 296 p.

Leder, Drew. *Spiritual Passages: Embracing Life's Sacred Journey (Inner Workbook).* New York: Tarcher/Putnam, 1997. 296 p.

Lederer, Richard. *Wholly Holy Bloopers.* Anguished English. Wyrick and Company, 1987.

Lee, Ramonia L. 1992. *"Healing Connections: Ethnic Perspectives on Spirituality and Mental Health."* Aging & Spirituality. http://www.asaging,org/networks/forsa/a&s92.html

Levin, Jeffrey S. *Religion in Aging and Health: Theoretical Foundations and Ethodological Frontiers.* Thousand Oaks, CA: Sage, 1994. 253 p.

Maitland, David J. *Aging as Counterculture: a Vocation for the Later Years.* New York: Pilgrim Press, 1990. 185 p.

Mathieu, Andre. *Toward a Spirituality of Aging.* 3 September 2001. http://www.cptryon.org/compassion/win96/spirit.html.

Maves, Paul B. *Faith for the Older Years.* Minneapolis, MN: Augsburg, 1986. 189 p.

Melia, S. Older women find that prayer matures along with them. *Aging and Spirituality. Spring 2001.* http://www.asaging.org/networks/forsa/a&s-124.html

Missine, Leo E. *Reflections on Aging: A Spiritual Guide.* Liguori, MO: Liguori, 1990. 112 p.

Moberg, David O. "Spiritual well-being defined." *Aging & Spirituality* 9:1 (Spring 1997). 8 p.

Perry, Robert. *About Stress.* 4 November 2001. http://www.robertperry.freeseerve.co.uk/aboutstress.htm.

Perschbacher Melia, Susan. *Older Women Find That Prayer Matures Along With Them.* 3 September 2001. http://asaging.org/networks/forsa/a&s-124.htm.

Ramsey, Janet L., and Rosemary Blieszner. *Spiritual Resiliency in Older Women: Models of Strength for Challenges Through the Life Span.* Thousand Oaks, CA: Sage, 1999. 180 p.

Revell, Albert A. *Caring for Seniors.* Newmarket, Ontario: York-Simcoe Ministries, 1992. 168 p.

Seeber, James J. *Spiritual Maturity in the Later Years.* New York, NY: Haworth, 1990. 196 p.

Siegel, B. *Love, Medicine and Miracles: Lessons Learned about Self-Healing from a Surgeon's Experience with Exceptional Patients.* Harperperennial Library, June 1990. 256 p.

Simmons, Henry Co. *Pastoral Responses to Older Adults and Their Families: An Annotated Bibliography.* NY: Greenwood, 1992. 218 p.

Smith, Gary. *Stress Reduction Tips.* 2001, 3 November 2001. http://wiwi.essortment.com/stressreduction_rhef.htm

Thomas, Eugene L. *Aging and the Religious Dimension.* Westport, CT: Auburn House, 1994.

Thomas L. Eugene, and Susan A. Eisenhandler, eds. *Religion, Belief and Spirituality in Late Life.* New York, NY: Springer Publishing, 1999. 221 p.

Vinall, Phil. *Praise the Spirit for Your Health.* CBS Health Watch. June 2001. 4 November 2001. http://cbshealthwatch.medscape.com/cx/viewarticle/217649_print.

Waxman, B.F. (1999). *Nature, Spirtuality and Later Life in Literature: An Essay on the Romanticism of Older Writers.* Gerontologist, 39 (5) pp. 516-524.

Wilson, Steve. *Laughter Clubs Are a Big Hit With the Elder-ish.*

Wilson, Steve. *Humor and Healing: The Invisible Weapon.* 1996.

Woodward, Jan. *Doctor Prescribes Humor for a Healthy Life.* Abilene Reporter-News. 1998. 11 November 2001. http://www.repoternews.com/local/heart0514.htm.

Wright, K. *Breaking the Rules: Removing the Obstacles to Effortless High Performance.* CPM Publishing. 1998. 305 p.

Index

A

B

N

S

Give *Field Guide for Families* to
Your Friends, Colleagues and Loved Ones

CHECK YOUR LOCAL BOOKSTORE OR ORDER HERE

YES, I want _____ copies of *A Field Guide For Families* at $15.95 each, plus $4 shipping per book (Connecticut residents please add $0.95 sales tax per book). Canadian orders must be accompanied by a postal money order in U.S. funds. Allow 15 days for delivery.

My check or money order for $_____ is enclosed.

Please charge my credit card in the amount of $_____.
Visa   MasterCard   American Express
Card #_____ Exp. Date_____
Signature_____

Bill To:
Name_____Phone (   )_____
Address_____Email:_____
Address_____
City/State/Zip_____

Ship To:
Name_____Phone (   )_____
Address_____Email:_____
Address_____
City/State/Zip_____

Please make your check payable and return to:
Life Design
Post Office Box 617
Niantic, CT 06357-0617
Fax orders to: (860) 691-0573

A Field Guide For Families is available at special quantity discounts for bulk purchases for sales promotions, premiums, fund-raising or educational use. Special editions can be created to fit specific needs. The author is available for training workshops, coaching, and speaking engagements. Contact Life Design at

(860) 691-0576 or www.lifedesigncoach.com for details.